BOY SCOUTS OF AMERICA
MERIT BADGE SERIES

SPACE EXPLORATION

Requirements

1. Tell the purpose of space exploration and include the following:
   a. Historical reasons
   b. Immediate goals in terms of specific knowledge
   c. Benefits related to Earth resources, technology, and new products

2. Design a collector's card, with a picture on the front and information on the back, about your favorite space pioneer. Share your card and discuss four other space pioneers with your counselor.

3. Build, launch, and recover a model rocket.* Make a second launch to accomplish a specific objective. (Rocket must be built to meet the safety code of the National Association of Rocketry. See the "Model Rocketry" chapter.) Identify and explain the following rocket parts.
   a. Body tube
   b. Engine mount
   c. Fins
   d. Igniter
   e. Launch lug
   f. Nose cone
   g. Payload
   h. Recovery system
   i. Rocket engine

*If local laws prohibit launching model rockets, do the following activity: Make a model of a NASA rocket. Explain the functions of the parts. Give the history of the rocket.

4. Discuss and demonstrate each of the following:
   a. The law of action-reaction
   b. How rocket engines work
   c. How satellites stay in orbit
   d. How satellite pictures of Earth and pictures of other planets are made and transmitted

5. Do TWO of the following:
   a. Discuss with your counselor an unmanned space exploration mission and an early manned mission. Tell about each mission's major discoveries, its importance, and what we learned from it about the planets, moons, or regions of space explored.
   b. Using magazine photographs, news clippings, and electronic articles (such as from the Internet), make a scrapbook about a current planetary mission.
   c. Design an unmanned mission to another planet or moon that will return samples of its surface to Earth. Name the planet or moon your spacecraft will visit. Show how your design will cope with the conditions of the planet's or moon's environment.

6. Describe the purpose, operation, and components of ONE of the following:
   a. Space shuttle
   b. International Space Station

7. Design an inhabited base located on the Moon or Mars. Make drawings or a model of your base. In your design, consider and plan for the following:
   a. Source of energy
   b. How it will be constructed
   c. Life-support system
   d. Purpose and function

8. Discuss with your counselor two possible careers in space exploration that interest you. Find out the qualifications, education, and preparation required and discuss the major responsibilities of those positions.

Contents

Why Explore Space? 7

Our Steps Into Space 13

Model Rocketry 23

The Way Things Work 33

Planetary Exploration 43

Near-Earth Space Habitats 57

Planetary Bases and Settlements in Space 75

Careers in Space Exploration 81

The Greatest Adventure 87

Space Exploration Resources 88

An astronaut uses a camera while working on the International Space Station.

SPACE EXPLORATION   5

NASA artist's concept of Pluto-Kuiper Express

Why Explore Space?

Space is mysterious. We explore space for many reasons, not least because we don't know what is out there, it is vast, and humans are full of curiosity. Each time we send explorers into space, we learn something we didn't know before. We discover a little more of what is there.

When you are on a hike, have you ever wondered what lies around the next bend in the trail, or beyond the next ridge, or down in the valley below? If so, then you will understand the thrill of sending a spacecraft to a world no human has ever seen.

Historical Reasons

Space has beckoned us, from early observers such as the Aztecs, Greeks, and Chinese; to 15th-century seafarers like Christopher Columbus and 17th-century astronomers including Galileo Galilei; to today's Boy Scouts. The stars and planets in the sky have helped us shape our beliefs, tell time, guide our sailing ships, make discoveries, invent devices, and learn about our world.

When electricity, airplanes, rockets, and computers came on the scene, some people realized it would be possible to put machines and people into space. No longer would we be limited to observing the wonders of space from the ground. Now we could enter and explore this curious environment. The "final frontier" could be opened.

However, it proved complicated and expensive to build a rocket to put objects into orbit around the Earth. In the mid-20th century, only two countries had the knowledge, workforce, and money to do it—the Soviet Union and the United States. The Soviet Union (USSR) showed its might by launching a small sphere into orbit. The Soviets' success with *Sputnik 1* in 1957 began the "space race" between the two countries.

Scientists got a big surprise in 2000 when new pictures of Mars showed hundreds of fresh gullies. The gullies suggest water has recently rushed down hillsides on Mars—a planet we have long believed was a dusty-dry desert.

WHY EXPLORE SPACE?

Apollo 15 astronaut Jim Irwin sets up the first Lunar Roving Vehicle on the Moon.

For more than 10 years, the United States and the Soviet Union competed by launching vehicles, animals, and people into space. The United States achieved its goal of landing men on the Moon by the end of the 1960s. Meanwhile, the Soviet Union built space stations to have a permanent presence in space. (See the chart called "Early Manned Spaceflight Programs" for more details about these early missions.)

We learned many new things from space missions focusing on science and education. Astronauts collected rocks from the Moon and did medical and scientific experiments above Earth's atmosphere. Unmanned spacecraft visited other planets. People watched on television as an astronaut hit a golf ball on the Moon and when a rover sniffed at a Martian rock. Space looked like fun!

Early Manned Spaceflight Programs

Program	Country	Years	Major Accomplishments
Vostok	USSR	1961–63	First manned spaceflight (Yuri Gagarin in *Vostok 1*, 1961); first woman in space (Valentina Tereshkova in *Vostok 6*, 1963)
Mercury	U.S.	1961–63	First U.S. manned suborbital flight (Alan Shepard in *Freedom 7*, 1961); first U.S. manned orbital flight (John Glenn in *Friendship 7*, 1962)
Voskhod	USSR	1964–65	First "spacewalk" or extravehicular activity (Alexei Leonov in *Voskhod 2*, March 1965)
Gemini	U.S.	1965–66	First U.S. extravehicular activity (Edward White in *Gemini 4*, June 1965); first docking of two spacecraft in orbit (Neil Armstrong and David Scott in *Gemini 8* with unmanned Agena rocket, 1966)
Soyuz	USSR	1967– (Russia continues to use the Soyuz rocket)	First extravehicular transfer of crew members from one spacecraft to another (Yevgeny Khrunov and Aleksei Yeliseyev from *Soyuz 5* to *Soyuz 4*, 1969)
Apollo	U.S.	1968–72	First manned orbit of the Moon (Frank Borman, James Lovell, and William Anders in *Apollo 8*, 1968); first manned lunar landing (Neil Armstrong and Buzz Aldrin in *Apollo 11*, 1969); five other successful manned lunar landings (*Apollos 12* and *14–17*, 1969–72)
Salyut	USSR	1971–86	First space station; first extensive photography of Earth from space; record-breaking endurance flight of 237 days (aboard *Salyut 7*, 1984–1985)
Skylab	U.S.	1973–74	First U.S. space station; three American crews stayed for 28, 59, and 84 days, the last setting a U.S. space-endurance record; first pictures of solar activity taken above Earth's atmosphere (175,000 pictures of the Sun made from Skylab)
Apollo-Soyuz	U.S.-USSR	1975	First international docking in space (Thomas Stafford, Deke Slayton, and Vance Brand in *Apollo 18*; Alexei Leonov and Valery Kubasov in *Soyuz 19*, July 1975)

Why Explore Space?

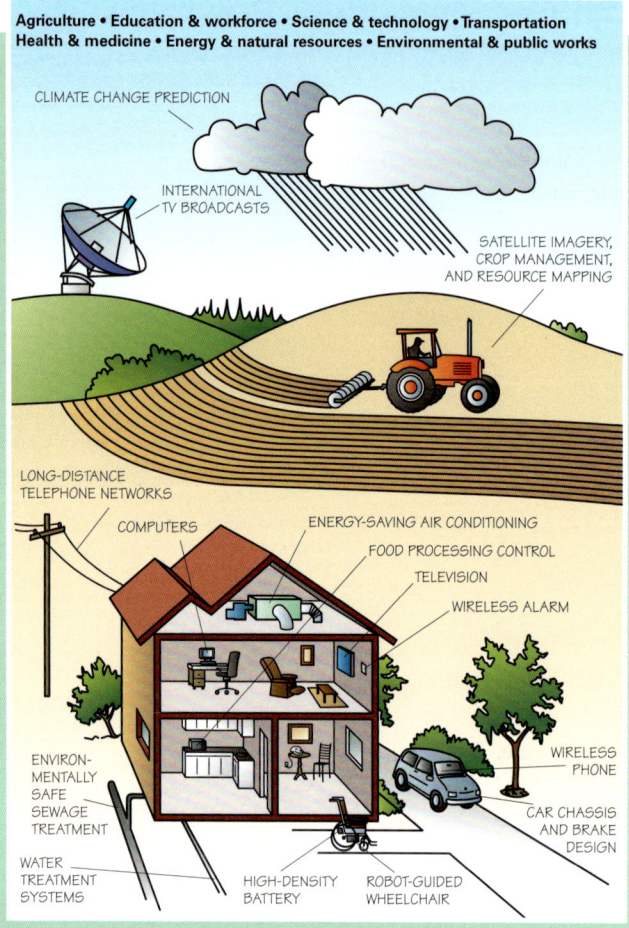

New materials, products, and technologies coming from the space program are called "spinoffs." Spinoffs from the space exploits of the National Aeronautics and Space Administration (NASA) include portable coolers, scratch-resistant lenses, self-righting life rafts, water treatment systems, virtual reality simulators, smoke detectors, cordless tools, firefighter suits made of flame-retardant materials, "cool suits" to lower a patient's body temperature, programmable pacemakers, and voice-controlled wheelchairs.

Current Benefits

Some business people looked beyond the fun and adventure of space exploration. They saw space as a chance to make money and satisfy society's needs. The commercial satellite industry blossomed in the 1980s.

Today, our ability to place satellites in orbit gives us many benefits. Seeing Earth's atmosphere from space, meteorologists can forecast weather and warn people of dangerous storms more accurately than ever before. Looking down on the land and the ocean from space, we have found natural resources and seen disturbing evidence of their careless destruction. Communication satellites help tie the world's population together, carrying video, telephone, computer, and Internet data for individuals, schools, governments, and businesses. Military satellites provide intelligence of vital interest to our armed forces and national security.

We have new medicines and medical devices thanks to the astronauts' experiences and experiments in space. With the construction of the International Space Station (see "Near-Earth Space Habitats") we are learning how to build structures in the vacuum of space. In the future, such structures could serve as manufacturing facilities for "out of this world" products or as hotels for thrill-seeking tourists.

> Any small nickel-iron asteroid contains trillions of dollars' worth of valuable metals. For more about asteroids, see the *Astronomy* merit badge pamphlet.

Humanity's Future

Space is about the future. The people who work in space-related projects—engineers and scientists, doctors and teachers, corporations and entrepreneurs—are seeking to improve the future of humanity.

Once we are able to carry people and cargo cheaply into space, we could establish communities in space stations and on the Moon and Mars. We could harness the Sun's energy by using solar-powered satellites to provide clean, reliable electricity to everyone on Earth. We could mine the Moon and asteroids for valuable minerals and metals rarely found on Earth. The far side of the Moon would be an excellent site for astronomical observatories.

Earth is only so big and it has only so many resources—resources that our ever-growing population is using up. Spreading humanity among the stars is a magnificent dream. After you read this pamphlet and earn the Space Exploration merit badge, perhaps you will do or discover something that could lead the way to the stars.

Our Steps Into Space

In 11th-century China, inventors and scholars developed gunpowder. One Chinese scholar packed a tube with gunpowder and sealed off one end. When the gunpowder was ignited, the tube shot forward and sometimes it would explode. People were hurt and property was destroyed during these experiments. Then someone realized this "fire work" could become a weapon, and the fire arrow was invented.

The first recorded use of rockets in war was in the year 1232 when the Mongols laid siege to the Chinese City of Kaifeng. The Chinese chased off the Mongols with a barrage of fire arrows. After the battle, the Mongols developed their own rockets. Some historians believe the Mongols introduced gunpowder and rockets to Europe.

From the 15th through the 17th centuries, cannons replaced rockets as military weapons. During the 18th century, rockets made a comeback thanks to William Congreve, an English inventor. His rockets helped the English win battles against Denmark, France, and Prussia. Francis Scott Key immortalized Congreve's weapons when he wrote of "the rockets' red glare" during the British attack on Fort McHenry in Baltimore Harbor during the War of 1812.

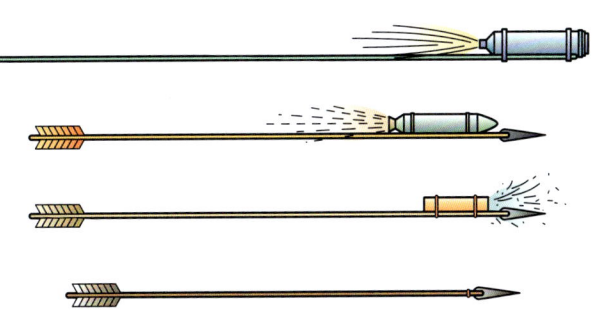

From bottom to top: The development of the Chinese "fire arrow"

SPACE EXPLORATION 13

The Dreamers

Although the rocket became an instrument of war, a few dreamers of the 19th and 20th centuries saw it as a method of transportation. *Could* people fly into space on a rocket? As the Industrial Revolution introduced new technology to the public, these dreamers used a new form of fiction—*science fiction*—to express their ideas of traveling beyond Earth.

Jules Verne (1828–1905) was born in Nantes, France. He went to Paris to study law. Instead, inspired by balloons, airships, and other new inventions, he began to write science fiction stories. He wrote *Around the World in Eighty Days* (1873), *Around the Moon* (1870), and *From the Earth to the Moon* (1865). In his novel *From the Earth to the Moon,* a giant cannon in Florida launches the space capsule. The astronauts circle the Moon and then land in the Pacific Ocean, where an American naval vessel recovers the crew and capsule. Verne told this story 100 years before the Apollo missions. Jules Verne is considered the father of modern science fiction.

H. G. Wells

H. G. Wells (1866–1946) was born in Bromley, England. He became a science teacher and wrote science fiction. He, too, kept up with the discoveries of his time. In the 1860s an Italian astronomer, Giovanni Schiaperelli, reported canals on Mars. A heated debate raged over the existence of a Martian civilization. H. G. Wells turned this debate into a novel, *The War of the Worlds* (1898). In the story, the Martians attack Earth because Mars is a dying planet and the Martians want Earth for their own. Wells wrote other stories involving space travel, such as *The First Men in the Moon* and *The Shape of Things to Come.*

Arthur C. Clarke

Arthur C. Clarke (1917–2008) wrote fiction and nonfiction for more than 60 years. He was born in Somerset County, England. In 1936, he joined the British Interplanetary Society. He published their journal and began to write science fiction stories. He served in the Royal Air Force during World War II and tested radar systems. After the war, he returned to school and received degrees in physics and mathematics. In 1945, he published a paper titled "Extraterrestrial Relays," which laid down the principles of modern communications satellites. Clarke's space-related works of fiction include the short story "The Sentinel," which was turned into the movie *2001: A Space Odyssey* (1968). His novels include *Earthlight, Islands in the Sky, The Sands of Mars,* and *Songs of a Distant Earth.*

Gene Roddenberry

Gene Roddenberry (1921–1991) was born in El Paso, Texas. He studied law for three years but switched to aeronautical engineering. In World War II, he joined the Air Force. He flew 89 combat missions and earned the Distinguished Flying Cross. Later he studied literature and moved to Los Angeles in 1949. He became a screenwriter for television. Then he developed and produced his own TV series, *Star Trek*. Premiering in 1966, this "Wagon Train to the Stars" became a classic. In the 1970s, a generation of "Trekkies" lobbied NASA to name the first space shuttle the *Enterprise*. When Roddenberry died, his remains were flown on a space shuttle mission, a tribute to the visionary who imagined a future where humanity peacefully traveled throughout the galaxy.

The Doers

After the Wright brothers ushered in the age of flight, three rocket scientists laid the foundations for the space age. Other "doers" were pilots who became astronauts.

Konstantin Tsiolkovsky (1857–1935) was a Russian teacher and scientist who wrote science fiction stories of interplanetary travel. He included real technical and scientific issues in his stories. He talked about using liquid propellant to power rocket ships. He also spoke of the need for spacesuits to protect people in the vacuum of space.

Dr. Robert H. Goddard (1882–1945), born in Worcester, Massachusetts, is considered the "father of modern rocketry." In 1907, while a student at Worcester Polytechnic Institute, he fired a rocket engine in the basement of the physics building, getting the attention of school officials. Seven years later, he patented his rocket inventions. In 1920, he published "A Method of Reaching Extreme Altitudes," in which he suggested using rockets to carry weather instruments aloft. Dr. Goddard developed a rocket using liquid fuel and launched a liquid-fueled rocket that went faster than the speed of sound. He developed the first practical automatic steering device for rockets.

Dr. Robert H. Goddard standing next to the rocket that would make the world's first liquid propellant rocket flight on March 16, 1926.

Our Steps Into Space

Dr. Wernher von Braun

Dr. Wernher von Braun (1912–1977) was born in Wirsitz, Germany. Inspired by a race car driver when he was 12, von Braun attached six rockets to a coaster wagon and lit the fuses. The wagon careened around his backyard, emitting a fountain of sparks. The commotion attracted the police, who took him into custody. Von Braun became interested in space exploration by reading the science fiction of Verne and Wells. Von Braun received his aerospace engineering degree and his Ph.D. in aerospace engineering in the early 1930s. He worked for the German army to build ballistic missile weapons. Familiar with Dr. Goddard's work, von Braun designed and built Germany's V-2 missile during World War II. At the end of the war, the U.S. Army realized the importance of Dr. von Braun's work. He was brought to the United States with more than 500 fellow scientists and with many V-2 missiles and components. He led the Army missile development program and launched the first U.S. satellite, *Explorer 1*, in 1958. His crowning achievement was the development of the Saturn class of rockets that carried the Apollo astronauts to the Moon.

Suborbital means "not completing a full orbit."

Alan Shepard (1923–1998) was born in East Derry, New Hampshire, and graduated from the Naval Academy. He saw action while flying off aircraft carriers during World War II. Shepard attended test-pilot school and was selected as one of the original *Mercury 7* astronauts in 1959. He was the first American to fly in space, on a Mercury *suborbital* mission in May 1961. Shortly after his flight, an inner-ear problem grounded him. An operation corrected the problem, allowing Shepard to lead the *Apollo 14* lunar-landing mission. He hit a golf ball on the Moon that traveled 900 yards—a record that still stands.

18   SPACE EXPLORATION

= OUR STEPS INTO SPACE

U.S. Sen. John Glenn (1921–), an Eagle Scout, was born in Cambridge, Ohio. He received his aerospace engineering degree, joined the Navy during World War II, and earned his wings as a Marine aviator. Glenn flew combat missions in World War II and Korea. He attended Navy test-pilot school and became one of the original Mercury astronauts. He was the first American to orbit Earth, in the *Friendship 7* Mercury capsule on February 20, 1962. He served as senator from Ohio for 24 years. Glenn returned to space on a space shuttle mission in 1998, becoming (at age 77) the oldest person to fly in space.

"The urge to explore the unknown is part of human nature. . . . It enriches our spirits and reminds us of the great potential for achievement within us all. The drive to develop the next frontier also has been a fundamental part of the heritage of the people of the United States."

—John Glenn

SPACE EXPLORATION 19

Our Steps Into Space

Neil Armstrong

Neil Armstrong (1930–) was born in Wapakoneta, Ohio, and earned his aerospace engineering degree from Purdue University. After serving as a naval aviator, he went to work for the government as an engineer, a test pilot, and then as an astronaut. Armstrong was selected as a Gemini astronaut and commanded the *Gemini 8* mission. Then he went into the Apollo program. On July 20, 1969, as commander of *Apollo 11*, Armstrong became the first man to set foot on the Moon.

Dr. Edwin E. "Buzz" Aldrin Jr. (1930–) was born in Montclair, New Jersey. He graduated third in his class at West Point, accepted an Air Force commission, and flew Sabre jets during the Korean War. He received his doctorate in astronautics from MIT, where he outlined the techniques to rendezvous and dock in space. NASA chose Aldrin to be an Apollo astronaut because of his education and test pilot experience. While at NASA, Aldrin developed and refined spaceflight techniques. He flew with Neil Armstrong in the *Eagle* lunar module and was the second human to set foot on the Moon. Before retiring from the Air Force, he commanded the test-pilot school at Edwards Air Force Base in California. Aldrin has been an outspoken supporter of space exploration and research.

> Was Buzz Aldrin's future preordained? His father was a student of Dr. Robert Goddard, and his mother's maiden name was Moon!

20   SPACE EXPLORATION

OUR STEPS INTO SPACE

Create a Collector's Card

For requirement 2, create a collector's card of your favorite space pioneer. You can copy or draw the person's face. Include appropriate biographical information. Give details of the person's contribution to spaceflight, including dates, missions, and other accomplishments.

Buzz Aldrin

Born January 20, 1930, New Jersey.
Graduate, U.S. Military Academy at West Point.
Flew Sabre jets during the Korean War.
U.S. Air Force test pilot.
Doctorate in space science from Massachusetts Institute of Technology.
Crew member of Apollo 11.
Second human to step foot on the Moon, July 20, 1969.

SPACE EXPLORATION   21

Model Rocketry

Model rocketry is a great way to learn about space exploration. The rocket you build won't reach space, but the science and technology that goes into your rocket is the same as NASA uses in launching giant rockets.

Model rockets are made of paper, balsa wood, plastic, glue, and paint. You build them with simple tools such as a modeling knife, sandpaper, scissors, rulers, and paintbrushes. Model rockets are powered by solid propellant rocket engines. Depending on the size and design of the rocket and the power of the engine, model rockets may fly only 50 feet high or up to a half mile in altitude.

You can purchase model rocket kits and engines online, through mail-order catalogs, and in toy and hobby shops. If you can borrow a rocket launcher, you can buy everything you need to complete requirement 3 for less than $15. If you buy or build your own launcher, the total cost for this requirement could be about $35 to $40.

> Though some toy stores sell model rocket kits, model rockets are anything but toys. They are powerful, and through misuse could harm animals, people, or property. By following the commonsense rules found later in this section, you can launch your rockets in complete safety over and over.

Building Your Rocket

If you have never built a model rocket before, it is best to start with a simple kit. The kit will consist of a body tube, nose cone, fins, engine mount, and parachute or some other recovery system that will gently lower your rocket to the ground at the end of its flight.

Model Rocketry

Engines must be purchased separately from the rocket. Be sure to buy the recommended engines for your kit. If you use engines that are too powerful, you may lose your rocket on its first flight.

Unless your rocket kit comes with preformed plastic fins, you will need to cut fins from sheets of balsa wood included in the kit. The instructions will tell you to sand the leading and trailing edges of the fins to look like the edge of a knife. Do a good job on this step, because sharp edges on the fins help the rocket slice cleanly through the air as it flies upward. Blunt fin edges cause *turbulence* (rough air) that robs your rocket of altitude.

Also do a good job painting the fins, and sanding and painting the nose cone if it, too, is made of balsa wood. Very smooth surfaces reduce friction with the air.

Stability-Checking Your Rocket

Check every rocket for stability before flying it. Stability checks before launch assure you that your rocket will fly properly. Unstable rockets tumble in the air and may head back toward the launchpad at high speed.

Stability checks are simple and require only a long piece of string, a piece of tape, and a few minutes of your time. To check a new model rocket, prepare the rocket for flight and insert a live engine. Tie a slipknot around the body of the rocket and slide it to the point where the rocket

Although you may be tempted to tear open the kit and begin slapping together the parts, take time to read all of the directions twice before starting. Reading all of the directions first will help you gather the tools and supplies needed for building your rocket.

is perfectly balanced on the string. Hold the string in one hand over your head, and begin to twirl your rocket as though you were spinning a lariat. As the rocket picks up speed, gradually play out the string until the rocket is about 6 to 8 feet away. If you are not tall, you may want to stand on a chair at this point.

If your rocket is stable, it will travel around you without tumbling. The nose cone will point into the air and the tail end will follow. If the tail end goes first or if the rocket tumbles, your rocket may be dangerous to fly. You can correct this situation by putting on larger fins or adding weight to the rocket's nose with a lump of clay.

Launching Your Rocket

When your rocket is ready for its first flight, you must choose a proper launching site. Your launching site should be a large field that is free of power and telephone lines, trees, buildings, or any other structures that might snag a returning rocket. Choose a field away from airports.

You will need a launchpad. Perhaps you can borrow a launchpad from a local model-rocket club, or join the members on a day when they are launching rockets. If not, you can either buy a launchpad kit or build your own. A simple launchpad can be built from a block of wood, a blast deflector made from a

MODEL ROCKETRY

Not all cities and towns permit model rocket launches. Check with your local fire department or police to find out about local regulations governing model rocket launches. You may have to travel to a rural area to find a launch site. Or you may choose to complete the alternate to requirement 3.

Directions for safe launching of your rocket will come with your rocket kit. Follow these instructions carefully.

flattened metal can, and a straight rod. Rods made specifically for rocket launchers are best and inexpensive. Buy one where you get your rocket supplies.

Your launch system should be electric. It must have a switch that closes only when you press it and then opens again automatically. It also should have a master switch, or you should be able to disconnect the batteries while you set up your next flight. The wires from your batteries (about 6 volts) should extend about 15 feet to small "alligator" clips at the ends. These clips will be attached to the wires of the igniter. *Never use fuses or matches to ignite your rocket.*

> Some kits may come with payload sections for carrying raw eggs or insects. **Never send up animals other than insects in your rockets.** An insect's strong outer skeleton protects it from launch stresses, but mammals and other animals with backbones will feel much discomfort and possibly die from the experience.

Accomplishing a Launch Objective

After you have made your first launch, make a second launch with a specific objective in mind. You might try to spot-land the rocket within a 50-foot circle. That isn't as easy as it sounds. You must make allowances for wind drift and aim your rocket accordingly.

Another objective might be to carry a payload aloft and recover it safely. Several rocket kits come with payload sections for carrying raw eggs or insects.

Still another objective would be to launch a small camera on your rocket to take a picture of the launch site from high altitude. Specially designed cameras are available for model rockets.

Model Rocket Safety Code*

1. **Materials.** I will use only lightweight, nonmetal parts for the nose, body, and fins of my rocket.
2. **Motors.** I will use only certified, commercially made model rocket motors, and will not tamper with these motors or use them for any purposes except those recommended by the manufacturer.
3. **Ignition System.** I will launch my rockets with an electrical launch system and electrical motor igniters. My launch system will have a safety interlock in series with the launch switch, and will use a launch switch that returns to the "off" position when released.
4. **Misfires.** If my rocket does not launch when I press the button of my electrical launch system, I will remove the launcher's safety interlock or disconnect its battery, and will wait 60 seconds after the last launch attempt before allowing anyone to approach the rocket.
5. **Launch Safety.** I will use a countdown before launch, and will ensure that everyone is paying attention and is a safe distance of at least 15 feet away when I launch rockets with D motors or smaller, and 30 feet when I launch larger rockets. If I am uncertain about the safety or stability of an untested rocket, I will check the stability before flight and will fly it only after warning spectators and clearing them away to a safe distance.
6. **Launcher.** I will launch my rocket from a launch rod, tower, or rail that is pointed to within 30 degrees of the vertical to ensure that the rocket flies nearly straight up, and I will use a blast deflector to prevent the motor's exhaust from hitting the ground. To prevent accidental eye injury, I will place launchers so that the end of the launch rod is above eye level or will cap the end of the rod when it is not in use.
7. **Size.** My model rocket will not weigh more than 1,500 grams (53 ounces) at liftoff and will not contain more than 125 grams (4.4 ounces) of propellant or 320 N-sec (71.9 pound-seconds) of total impulse. If my model rocket weighs more than one pound (453 grams) at liftoff or has more than four ounces (113 grams) of propellant, I will check and comply with Federal Aviation Administration regulations before flying.

MODEL ROCKETRY

8. **Flight Safety.** I will not launch my rocket at targets, into clouds, or near airplanes, and will not put any flammable or explosive payload in my rocket.
9. **Launch Site.** I will launch my rocket outdoors, in an open area at least as large as shown in the accompanying table, and in safe weather conditions with wind speeds no greater than 20 miles per hour. I will ensure that there is no dry grass close to the launch pad, and that the launch site does not present risk of grass fires.
10. **Recovery System.** I will use a recovery system such as a streamer or parachute in my rocket so that it returns safely and undamaged and can be flown again, and I will use only flame-resistant or fireproof recovery system wadding in my rocket.
11. **Recovery Safety.** I will not attempt to recover my rocket from power lines, tall trees, or other dangerous places.

Launch Site Dimensions

Installed Total Impulse (N-sec)	Equivalent Motor Type	Minimum Site Dimensions (ft.)
0.00–1.25	$1/4$A, $1/2$A	50
1.26–2.50	A	100
2.51–5.00	B	200
5.01–10.00	C	400
10.01–20.00	D	500
20.01–40.00	E	1,000
40.01–80.00	F	1,000
80.01–160.00	G	1,000
160.01–320.00	Two Gs	1,500

Revision of February 2001

*Approved by the National Association of Rocketry (NAR), *http://www.nar.org/NARmrsc.html*

SPACE EXPLORATION

Rocket Parts

The **body tube** is the barrel of the rocket. It holds the engine, the recovery device, and the payload. The rocket's fins and launch lug are mounted to the body tube.

The **engine mount** is a small tube that is glued to the inside of the body tube. The engine mount provides a sturdy place for inserting the rocket engine.

Rocket **fins** are the main stability device of the rocket. Their function is similar to that of feathers on an arrow.

Igniters are small wires that are inserted into the nozzle of a rocket engine. When electricity is passed through the wire, the wire heats, and chemicals coating the wire ignite. This, in turn, ignites the rocket engine. The igniter wires are blasted out the nozzle when the engine propellants start burning.

Before fins can stabilize a rocket, the rocket must be moving through the air. The **launch lug** is a small straw mounted to the side of the body tube. The lug slides over the rod on the launchpad, and the rod stabilizes the rocket until the fins are able to take over (which happens in a fraction of a second).

The **nose cone** is fitted at the upper end of the rocket. Its purpose is to divide the air smoothly so the rocket can travel through the air with little turbulence. Nose cones are usually tapered to a point.

Payloads that can be carried on model-rocket flights include small cameras, radio transmitters, and raw eggs. Payloads carried on space rockets include satellites, spacecraft bound for other planets, scientific experiments, and astronauts.

Model rockets can be recovered in many ways. **Recovery systems** may be parachutes that are stored inside the body tube and ejected automatically by the rocket engine near the time the rocket reaches its maximum altitude. Streamers also are used for recovery. They slow the rocket as it falls back. Other recovery systems are helicopter-type rotors or wings for gliding landings.

The **rocket engine** is the power plant of your model rocket. An engine consists of a cylinder, called the *casing,* that holds the solid propellant. The upper end of the casing usually has a *plug* and the lower end has a *nozzle.* The nozzle is a small opening through which the burning gases escape. The nozzle makes the gases travel at high speeds when they exit, much the same way the nozzle on a garden hose makes water squirt farther when the hole is smaller. Inside the engine are

= MODEL ROCKETRY

the solid propellants. The propellants have oxygen built into their chemistry. This enables them to burn even in outer space, where there is no outside oxygen. (Rocket engines are different from jet engines. Jet engines must take in air from the atmosphere to burn their fuel.)

Model rocket parts

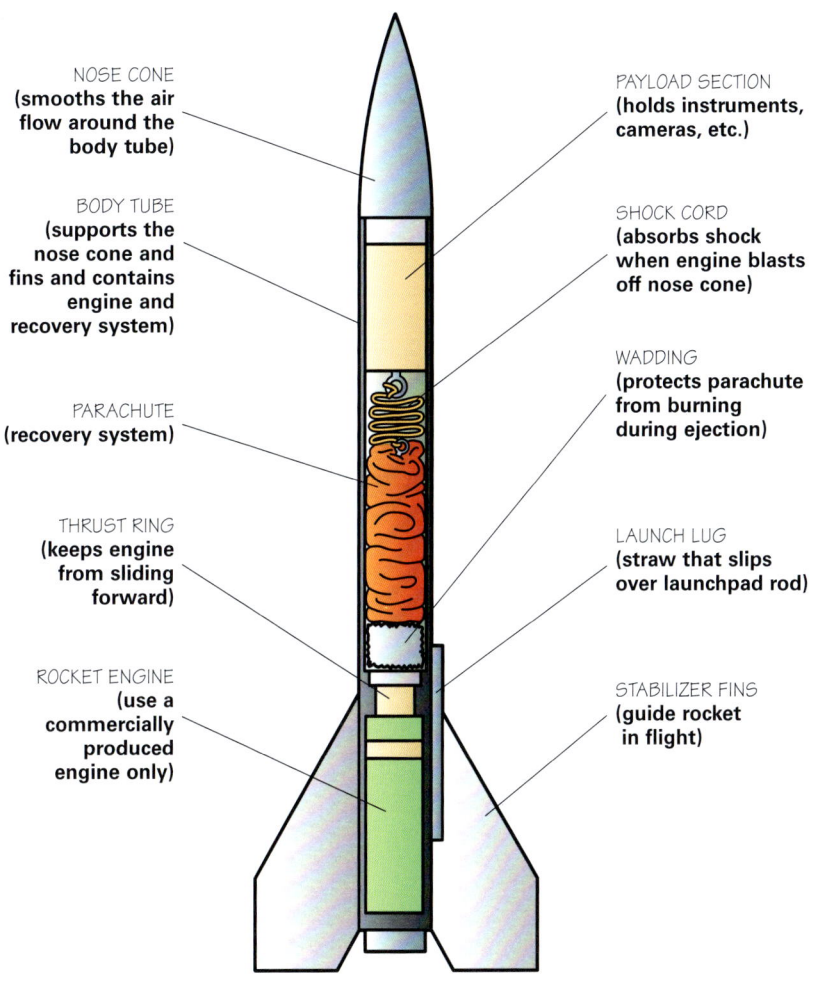

SPACE EXPLORATION 31

A rocket must accelerate to more than 25,000 miles per hour to completely escape Earth's gravity and fly off into space.

The Way Things Work

Space exploration has been a reality since the late 1950s. Space-age words such as *rocket, satellite,* and *orbit* have become part of nearly everyone's vocabulary. While many people use these words, few really understand the important concepts behind them, such as how a rocket works, how a satellite stays in orbit, or how pictures taken of other planets arrive on Earth.

Physical Laws of Space Flight

In the 17th century a great English mathematician and scientist named Sir Isaac Newton developed the basics of modern physics. He formed the theories of gravitation when he was only 23 years old. Some 20 years later, he presented his three laws of motion. These three laws explain how a rocket is able to work and how satellites and spacecraft are able to get into orbit and stay there.

Newton's Three Laws of Motion

1. An object in motion tends to stay in motion, and an object at rest tends to stay at rest, unless the object is acted upon by an outside unbalanced force.

2. Force equals mass times acceleration.

3. For every action there is an equal and opposite reaction.

These three laws of motion help make it easier to understand how rockets, satellites, and spacecraft work.

The First Law

Conventional rockets carry propellant, which consists of both fuel and *oxidizer*. For a rocket to work in space, it must carry oxygen or a chemical that contains oxygen for the fuel to burn.

Newton's first law is a simple statement of fact. To make an object move, an unbalanced force must be exerted on that object. An unbalanced force is important because forces that are balanced cancel each other out. Imagine two football players pushing against each other. If they exert equal force, they stay in the same place. If one player exerts more force than the other, the weaker player is pushed backward.

It is the same with a rocket. When a rocket is sitting on the launchpad, gravity tries to pull the rocket downward. The structure around the rocket holds the rocket up. Each exerts a force that balances the other, and the rocket stays at rest on the launchpad. When the rocket engine fires, the rocket exerts a greater force than the pull of Earth's gravity. It begins to climb slowly upward. As the rocket gets higher and farther from Earth's surface, the force due to gravity is less, and therefore the rocket climbs faster.

Once in outer space, the rocket goes into orbit around Earth and the engine stops firing. The rocket continues to move because forces have again become balanced. Its motion balances the pull of gravity. (See the section "How Satellites Stay in Orbit.") To bring the rocket back to Earth, those balanced forces must again be unbalanced. This time, the rocket engine fires in the direction of motion to start slowing the rocket. When this happens, gravity brings the rocket back down into the atmosphere.

The Second Law

Newton's second law refers to the amount of force (thrust) a rocket engine produces. Burning rocket propellants produce flames, smoke, and gas. These shoot out of the engine as exhaust to produce the thrust.

The amount of thrust depends on two things—mass and acceleration. *Mass* is the total amount of matter contained in the fire, smoke, and gas. The more matter present, the greater the thrust produced. *Acceleration* refers to how fast the exhaust is expelled from the rocket engine. The greater the acceleration, the greater the thrust.

Putting mass and acceleration together gives the simple formula $F = ma$. Keeping this formula in mind, a rocket designer should try to make both the burned mass (m) and the acceleration (a) as large as possible to get the maximum thrust (force, F). A heavier rocket, however, requires more thrust to lift it off the ground.

The Third Law

Newton's third law is the most familiar to people. It is sometimes called the *law of action-reaction*. Imagine you are a firefighter holding a fire hose. When the water is turned on, it explodes out of the hose and douses the fire. The motion of the water is an *action*. At the same time the water is thrown from the hose, the hose produces a strong recoil (kick) on your body, pushing you backward. This is a *reaction*. The reaction is in the opposite direction from the action and is equal in its force.

How Rockets Are Propelled

Rockets are driven by engines that obey Newton's three laws of motion. While a rocket sits on the launchpad, it is in a state of rest because all forces are balanced. When the rocket engine fires, forces become unbalanced (first law). As exhaust rushes downward out of the engine, an upward thrust is produced because of action-reaction (third law). The strength of that thrust is determined by the amount of matter expelled by the engine and how fast the matter is expelled (second law).

Forcing the exhaust through a small opening called a nozzle increases the speed of the exhaust, producing more thrust. Imagine using a garden hose with a nozzle attachment. With the nozzle wide open, the water streams out and lands a few feet away. By shrinking the nozzle opening, you force the water to move faster and it lands farther away. The greater the velocity, the greater the thrust. You can feel the thrust of the garden hose if you hold it. The same principle applies to rocket engines.

Rocket engines come in many varieties, based on the type of fuel used. Some types of engines used on today's spacecraft include solid propellant engines, liquid propellant engines, hybrid engines, and ion engines. Nuclear engines, solar sails, mass drivers, and other kinds of "futuristic" engines are being studied or developed.

Solid Propellant Rocket Engines

The first rocket engines, invented in China hundreds of years ago, used solid propellant. A solid propellant is a chemical compound in powder form that will burn but not explode. The powder is burned at one end of a tube, and the exhaust escapes out the other end.

The movement of a balloon when air is released from it also demonstrates the third law of motion. In the case of the balloon, what is the action? What is the reaction?

Solid propellant engines have three advantages: simplicity, low cost, and safety. However, they have two disadvantages: the engine can't be stopped or restarted after the fuel begins to burn, and thrust cannot be changed during the burn. Solid fuel rockets are used for short tasks, like shooting missiles or boosting the space shuttle. To have more control over a rocket, liquid propellant engines must be used.

Liquid Propellant Rocket Engines

In this engine type, the fuel and oxidizer are liquids carried in separate tanks. The fuel and oxidizer are pumped into a combustion chamber where the fuel is burned. The exhaust is forced out of the combustion chamber through a nozzle and produces thrust. The nozzle can be tilted to point the thrust in different directions, creating an effective way to steer the rocket.

Liquid hydrogen (fuel) and liquid oxygen (oxidizer) are the best liquid propellants for rockets. They must be kept very, very cold, so the fuel tanks are carefully insulated. These super-cold fluids also are used to cool the super-heated parts of the engine, like the combustion chamber and the nozzle, allowing them to be made of thin metal. Using the liquids as a coolant system allows the weight of the rocket to be reduced.

Hybrid Propellant Rocket Engines

Hybrid engines combine a solid fuel with a liquid oxidizer. The solid fuel is contained within the combustion chamber. The oxidizer is fed into the combustion chamber from an oxidizer tank. The exhaust is forced through a nozzle, creating thrust.

Ion Rocket Engines

Ion rocket engines accelerate ions to produce thrust. Ions are created by stripping electrons from atoms. The propellant, usually xenon gas, is heated to extremely high temperature, which causes the xenon atom to give up an electron. The positively charged ion is passed over a positively charged plate that repels and accelerates the ion from the thrust chamber, at extremely high speeds.

Ion engines are the most efficient rocket engines in use today. They produce a low thrust, but they operate for a long time. This means they have a high thrust for the amount of fuel used. An ion engine proved itself on the probe *Deep Space 1*, launched in 1998 and powered by a first-of-its-kind ion engine. (See "Planetary Exploration" in the next section.)

For more about atoms, electrons, and ions, see the *Electricity* merit badge pamphlet.

When you try to push the same poles of two magnets together, the magnets will push each other away—action and reaction. An ion engine behaves similarly.

How Satellites Stay in Orbit

Isaac Newton reasoned that it was the force of gravity, not the absence of gravity, that kept the Moon in orbit around Earth. Artificial satellites also operate under the same Newtonian laws.

To explain Newton's reasoning, think about what happens when you throw a ball. Imagine you are standing in a big field and throw a baseball as hard as you can. The ball might travel 100 feet before gravity pulls the ball down to the ground.

Now imagine you are standing on Mount Everest. You throw the baseball and it travels parallel to Earth for some distance before it falls to Earth. Each time you throw the ball, you increase the thrust and the ball travels farther. If you could throw the ball fast enough (and if you ignore friction from the atmosphere), the ball would fall at exactly the same rate that the curve of Earth falls away from the ball. This situation is called *free fall*. The ball would continue traveling parallel to Earth's surface, achieving orbit. This is the basis for how satellites stay in orbit.

This photo, taken from the shuttle's aft (rear) flight deck windows, shows an astronaut from the space shuttle *Endeavour* trying to capture the Intelsat VI communications satellite.

The Way Things Work

At higher altitudes, where the vacuum of space is nearly complete, there is almost no drag and a satellite can stay in orbit for centuries.

All satellites ride on rockets to get into orbit. Satellites as large as several tons make it safely into orbit on a regular basis.

Rockets travel straight up at first. This is the quickest way to get the rocket through the thickest part of Earth's atmosphere. Once above the atmosphere, the rocket control mechanism brings the rocket to a course that is parallel to Earth's surface. The rocket then accelerates to the velocity needed for that satellite to remain in orbit. This velocity is determined by the weight of the satellite and the height of the orbit to be achieved.

Orbital velocity is the speed needed to reach a balance between gravity's pull on the satellite and the satellite's tendency to keep going. If the satellite moves too fast, it will escape from Earth, never coming back. If the satellite moves too slow, gravity will pull it back to Earth. At the correct speed, the satellite is in perpetual free fall.

> Because of this constant state of falling, the satellite and everything aboard is nearly weightless. That is why astronauts can float inside the space shuttle.

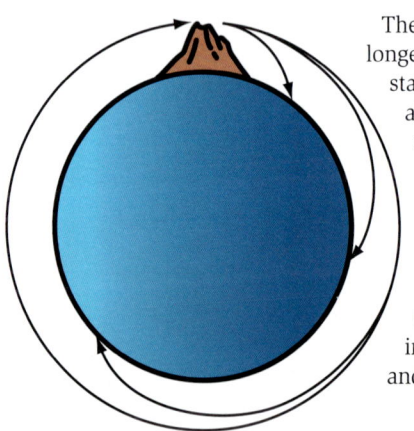

The higher the orbit, the longer the satellite can stay in orbit. At lower altitudes, a satellite runs into traces of Earth's atmosphere, which creates drag. The drag causes the orbit to decay (gradually fail) until the satellite falls back into the atmosphere and burns up.

The arrows represent baseballs thrown at different velocities.

SPACE EXPLORATION

THE WAY THINGS WORK

Space Pictures

Space pictures have evolved along with the digital technology of the computer, Internet, and cell phone. Early space pictures were made on film, which had to be returned to Earth and processed in the ordinary way. Early video was grainy and barely usable.

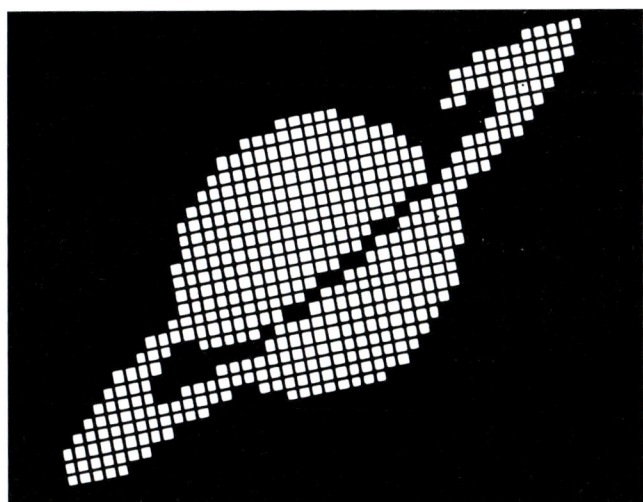

Images taken by spacecraft consist of many tiny squares called *pixels.* The picture of Saturn, *top,* is made of hundreds of thousands of pixels, shown (greatly exaggerated) at *bottom.*

SPACE EXPLORATION 39

THE WAY THINGS WORK

As space probes ventured farther into space, scientists needed a better way to record, store, and transmit pictures. Information scientists developed a coding system that treats each picture frame as a grid with numbered squares. Each square is a picture element—*pixel*, for short. Every pixel has its own address of numbers in the grid that gives the pixel's row and column. For example, the address of the pixel in row 01, column 01, is 01-01. The address of the pixel in row 16, column 10, is 16-10. (See the illustration.)

When a space probe's sensor views an object, it senses the brightness or shade of each pixel in the scene. Shades are measured on a *gray scale*, which is a gauge of the shades of gray from pure white to pure black.

Let's assume we have a simple gray scale with only five shades. Each shade is numbered. White is 01, light gray is 02, and so on to solid black, 05. The sensor assigns each pixel the number that corresponds to the shade sensed.

Tone Scale

01	White
02	Light Gray
03	Medium Gray
04	Dark Gray
05	Black

In this "smiley face" example, pixel 01-01 is white, and therefore is coded as 01-01-01. Pixel 06-02 is black. It is coded as 06-02-05. Pixel 06-06 is light gray. It is coded as 06-06-02.

40   SPACE EXPLORATION

These numbers are stored in a computer memory and then transmitted by radio to the waiting scientists. The receiving computer is programmed to arrange the pixels into a grid, show the correct shade of gray for each picture element, and reconstruct the picture row by row.

In early missions where the data transmission rate was slow and computer memory limited, it might take several minutes to display one picture frame. *Mariner 4,* when it photographed Mars in 1965, made images 200 x 200 pixels in size. Each complete image took nearly 9 hours to reach Earth. In contrast, the *Clementine* lunar mission in 1994 returned 2 million images in $2^1/_2$ months, averaging more than 1,000 images an hour. (These robot spacecraft are described in the next section, "Planetary Exploration.")

Placing three color filters (red, green, blue) over the pixels adds color to space pictures. Sometimes this filtering technique is used to create what is called a *false color image.* Studies have shown that certain plants will show a different color if infected by a disease, for instance. The same holds true for variations in water content, pollution, and other situations that interest the investigating scientist.

A farmer in North Dakota takes part in a program that gives him satellite imagery of his farm. He can see moisture content and decide when to plow and seed his crops. As the crops grow, he can tell if insecticides or fertilizers are required. The farmer can tell when his wheat is ripe and can be harvested. This is just one of many examples of how space pictures can improve everyday life.

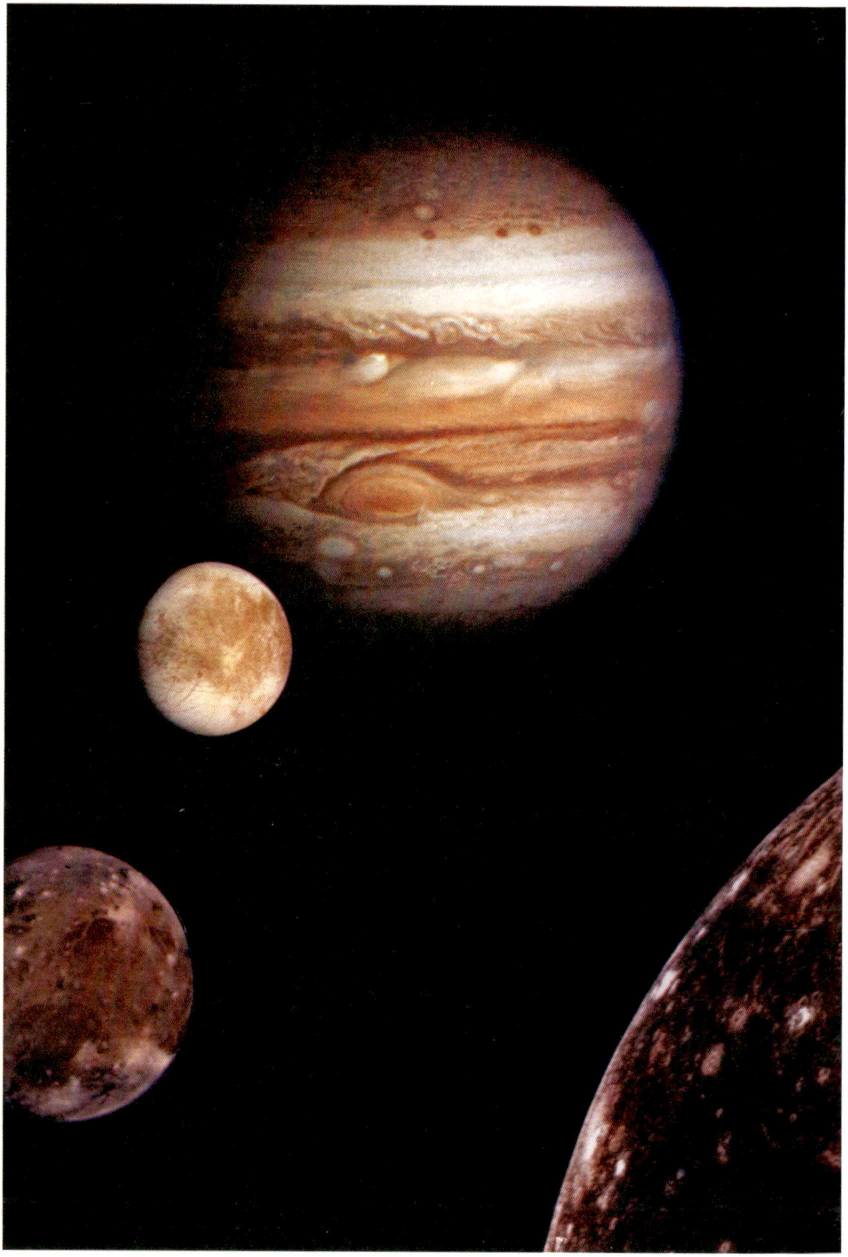

PLANETARY EXPLORATION

Planetary Exploration

Long ago, the Greeks noticed bright, starlike objects moving among the stars. These "wanderers" included the Sun, Moon, Mercury, Venus, Mars, Jupiter, and Saturn. People thought all these objects circled Earth, which was thought to be at the center of the universe.

In the 16th century, Nicolaus Copernicus determined that Earth was a planet, too, and that the six known planets went around (orbited) the Sun while the Moon circled Earth. Then, in 1610, Galileo Galilei turned a newly invented instrument—the telescope—toward the heavens. He looked at Jupiter, and what he saw astounded him.

Through the telescope, Jupiter was not a wandering point of light, but a round disk with four small starlets (moons) circling it. Earth's Moon was not a smooth shadowy ball, but a sphere pockmarked with craters and laced with cracks and ridges. Venus went through phases like the Moon, Saturn had bumps on its sides (the rings), and the Sun had spots on its surface. The worlds of outer space were more exciting than anyone had imagined.

Almost 350 years later, when people learned how to send objects—spacecraft—into space, a new era of exploration began. Scientific instruments and cameras could now be carried above the filtering effects of Earth's atmosphere, providing clearer views of outer space than ever before. Spacecraft could go to those faraway places Copernicus and Galileo barely knew.

For more about planets, moons, and stars, see the *Astronomy* merit badge pamphlet.

Space Probes: Tools of the Space Age

A *spacecraft* is any vehicle that flies in outer space, whether or not it carries people. An unmanned spacecraft is technically known as a *space probe*. Such probes have been used since the late 1950s to explore other worlds, large and small, in our solar system.

SPACE EXPLORATION 43

PLANETARY EXPLORATION

The space probe *Voyager 2*

Scientists or engineers might want to change the computer programs that tell the spacecraft what to do. When new commands are received, the spacecraft's computer stores the commands and executes them at the right time.

A space probe is a clever arrangement of mechanical and electronic parts packed together inside a sturdy, compact box or shell that is launched aboard a rocket. Once in space, the box opens and the various parts (components) begin to operate. Each group of components plays an important role toward accomplishing the mission—controlling the spacecraft, taking measurements of its surroundings, or communicating with people on Earth, thousands or millions of miles away.

Scientific instruments aboard a spacecraft detect and measure what's out there. Almost every probe carries one or more cameras to capture images of the object it visits. Some probes may have devices to measure radiation, temperature, and magnetic fields. Those that land on an alien surface may carry a miniature weather station and a scoop to sample the soil. Other devices may be designed to detect certain chemical elements or compounds, such as water.

A computer system stores commands that direct the other components to function and to control the craft. The computer also collects the information gathered by the instruments and gets it ready for transmission to Earth. When it is time to send the data to Earth, an antenna aims radio signals in the right direction. Another antenna receives signals from Earth.

To do all these things, a spacecraft needs a power supply. The probe may have solar cells to convert sunlight into electricity. Or it may have a nuclear-powered generator to provide electricity, especially if it is visiting a planet far from the Sun. Because outer space is extremely cold, some power goes to a heater that keeps the spacecraft at the right temperature for the computer, instruments, and other components to operate.

After the probe has been launched into space, altering its direction becomes necessary during millions of miles of travel. A set of small rockets (thrusters) is used to adjust the probe's course or "put on the brakes" if the probe must go into orbit around a planet or land on an alien surface.

PLANETARY EXPLORATION

> Another means of changing direction and increasing speed takes advantage of a large planet's gravity—a "slingshot" effect, known as *gravity assist*. With careful aim, a probe can be pulled toward the planet, whipped around, and then accelerated away in the desired direction. Spacecraft use the gravity-assist method to travel quickly to their destination while conserving precious fuel.

Unmanned Missions to the Moon

The Soviet Union reached the Moon first in early 1959 with its robot spacecraft *Luna 1*, which zoomed by at 3,100 miles above the lunar surface. More daring, the Soviets had *Luna 2* crash-land, becoming the first human-made object to touch the Moon. Then *Luna 3* took the first photographs of the far side of the Moon, which no one had ever seen before.

The first American lunar flyby was by *Pioneer 4* in March 1959. The probe passed within 37,300 miles of the Moon and went into orbit around the Sun. A series of probes failed to reach the Moon until *Rangers 7, 8,* and *9* succeeded spectacularly. They transmitted detailed pictures of the lunar surface before crash-landing in 1964 and 1965.

Next came the Surveyor and Lunar Orbiter programs, which had 10 probes visit the Moon successfully between 1966 and 1968. Five three-legged Surveyors landed softly on the Moon to test landing techniques, take close-up pictures of the surface, and study the nature of the soil. Five Lunar Orbiters orbited the Moon and photographed 99 percent of its surface, including the far side. Information from these lunar probes was crucial in choosing the best landing site for a manned mission.

Meanwhile, the Soviet Union continued to explore the Moon with the Zond series. Zond spacecraft flew around the Moon, took quality photographs, and returned to Earth.

Zond 5 was the only spacecraft to carry living creatures other than humans as far as the Moon. A payload of turtles, mealworms, plants, and other life-forms survived the trip and splashed down in the Indian Ocean in September 1968.

Clementine made this mosaic of the near side of the Moon in 1994. In this view, north is up. The bright crater near the bottom of the image is Tycho.

SPACE EXPLORATION

Planetary Exploration

> The next time you gaze at the Moon, think of all those robot spacecraft, as well as the relics of the Apollo manned missions, that lie silently on the lunar surface. Imagine being a scrap-metal dealer on the Moon.

After the Apollo program ended in 1975, not a single spacecraft traveled to the Moon for 15 years. The Japanese experienced limited success with a probe in 1990.

In 1994, the U.S. Department of Defense launched an experimental spacecraft named *Clementine* that orbited the Moon for 70 days, mapping its surface and detecting the possible presence of frozen water at the Moon's south pole. In 1998, *Lunar Prospector* mapped the lunar surface in more detail, measured magnetic and gravity fields, and studied geological events. After one year, it gave its life to science by intentionally crashing near the south pole in the hope of revealing water ice. Alas, astronomers observed no ice.

Unveiling Venus and Mercury

Mysterious Venus, whose surface hides from Earth-based telescopes under a shroud of clouds, was the first planet after Earth to be examined by an unmanned spacecraft. The United States had *Mariner 2*, after orbiting the Sun for almost a year, approach and fly by Venus in December 1962. The spacecraft reported the planet was over 900 degrees Fahrenheit, hotter than Mercury.

The Soviet Union was bolder with its Venera program, 16 probes that intensively explored Venus between 1961 and 1983. Venera was the first spacecraft to probe the planet's atmosphere, the first to land there, the first to photograph its surface, the first to analyze the soil, and the first to map the terrain. Starting with *Venera 4* (1967), the spacecraft was two probes, a carrier that stayed up high and a lander that dropped toward the surface. But the dense Venusian atmosphere crushed each lander before it could land. Eventually, *Venera 7* was built strong enough to safely descend. It lasted for 23 minutes on the surface of Venus in 1970.

Mercury photographed by *Mariner 10* in March 1974 as the spacecraft left the planet.

PLANETARY EXPLORATION

The United States then sent *Mariner 10*, which achieved two goals. Three months after launch in November 1973, the probe flew by Venus and took many measurements of the atmosphere. With assistance from Venus' gravity (like a slingshot), it sped onward to Mercury, the Sun's closest planet. *Mariner 10*, which photographed about 40 percent of Mercury's surface, has been the only probe to visit there to date.

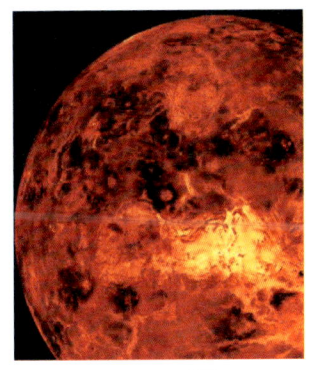

Magellan's view of Venus

In the 1980s, *Vega 1, Vega 2,* and *Magellan* visited Earth's "sister" planet. The Vegas, identical 36-foot-long probes from the Soviet Union, reached Venus in June 1985. They dropped a landing capsule onto the surface, released a balloon into the atmosphere, and then got slingshot by the planet to intercept Halley's Comet. The balloon carried instruments that measured atmospheric temperature, pressure, and wind speed. The lander took similar measurements and photographs, and analyzed the chemical makeup of the air and soil.

Magellan, about 20 feet tall and nearly 15 feet wide, was the first planetary spacecraft to be launched from the space shuttle (in May 1989). After entering a polar orbit around Venus in August 1990, *Magellan* spent more than four years mapping 98 percent of the hidden terrain using a powerful radar.

Magellan revealed the presence of large volcanoes, lava plains, and extremely long lava channels. It also discovered deformed, flattened mountains. We finally knew what lurked under Venus' clouds: a barren world.

Missions to the Red Planet

At the end of the 19th century, astronomer Percival Lowell focused a large telescope on Mars. He reported seeing canals on the Martian surface. People's imaginations soared, but scientists had to wait until 1965 before a spacecraft flew to the Red Planet. Pictures from *Mariner 4* revealed a Martian surface covered with craters. The probe's instruments found Mars had a thin atmosphere of mostly carbon dioxide. Not a single canal or other sign of life was spotted.

Mariner 9 was the first U.S. spacecraft to orbit another planet. When the probe arrived at Mars in November 1971, it found a dust storm enveloping the world. The probe was told to delay taking pictures of the surface, a wait that lasted

PLANETARY EXPLORATION

a couple of months before the dust settled. Eventually, after 349 days in orbit, *Mariner 9* had transmitted more than 7,000 images, covering over 80 percent of the Martian surface. Among notable features were river beds, massive extinct volcanoes, and a series of canyons that stretched more than 2,500 miles long, nearly as long as the continental United States. The probe found evidence of wind erosion, water erosion, weather fronts, clouds, and fog—but no life.

The Soviet Union turned its attention to Mars in the 1970s. Two probes of the Soviets' Mars series (the first failed to reach its destination) arrived in November 1971, a few weeks after *Mariner 9*. The *Mars 2* spacecraft released a lander that descended into the raging dust storm and crashed. However, the orbiter took photographs and studied the atmosphere and surface. *Mars 3*, which was identical to *Mars 2*, had better luck. The vehicle landed safely and transmitted the first television pictures of the Martian surface. That lasted for 20 seconds, then communication from the lander was lost.

Americans were excited when two Viking missions reached Mars in 1976. Each craft had two parts, an orbiter and a lander. *Viking 1* landed on July 20, 1976, while *Viking 2* settled on the other side of the planet six weeks later. While each orbiter took detailed photos and communicated with Earth, each lander stood on three legs with large circular footpads and performed its duties. A camera took the first close-up image of the Martian surface—a footpad and a bunch of rocks. More pictures followed and some were in color, revealing red boulders, red soil, and a pinkish sky. People were awestruck.

> The redness of the rocks and soil on Mars is due to the presence of iron oxide, which we know as rust. The sky looks pink because of the dust blown about by the wind.

The *Viking 1* lander dug these trenches on Mars.

48 SPACE EXPLORATION

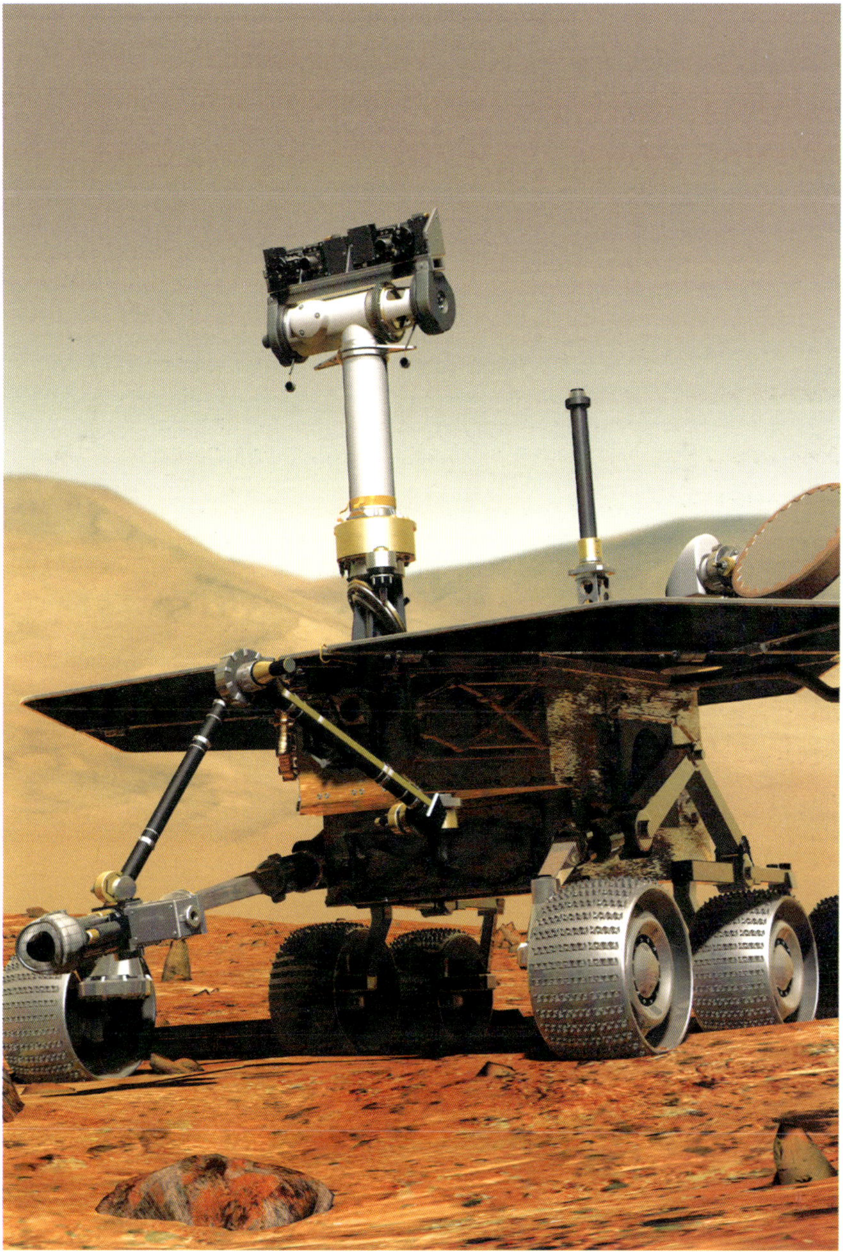

PLANETARY EXPLORATION

> Mars' giant canyon was named Valles Marineris in honor of the Mariner spacecraft. The canyon is three times as deep as the Grand Canyon. One of Mars' extinct volcanoes, Olympus Mons, is 15 miles high, the largest in the solar system.

Each Viking lander extended a long arm into the soil, scooped up samples, and dropped them into three chemical laboratories. The labs tested the soil to find chemicals that might come from a microscopic organism. One lab contained a mixture of nutrients for the microbes to eat that scientists jokingly called "chicken soup." But the results of all these experiments were inconclusive, the scientists decided. Everyone was disappointed, but there was still much to learn about Mars.

Mars Pathfinder was the next spacecraft to arrive safely, landing on July 4, 1997. The craft bounced onto the Martian surface, its fall from space cushioned by inflated airbags. The craft was shaped as a tetrahedron—four triangular sides—so that when it stopped bouncing, the three sides standing up would fall open like a flower.

Aboard was a small rover (two feet long and one foot high) named *Sojourner*. Powered by a solar panel on its back, the rover rolled down a ramp and traveled close enough to the nearest rock for one of its instruments to touch the rock and determine its composition. Then the rover visited other rocks, large and small, around the lander.

The rover was designed to last for seven days and the lander for 30 days; each operated for 83 days. For many, *Mars Pathfinder* was the most spectacular unmanned mission to date.

Two more probes are in operation around Mars at the time of this publication. *Mars Global Surveyor* arrived in September 1997. After establishing a nearly polar orbit, it began mapping the terrain in early 1999. Then *2001 Mars Odyssey* entered orbit in October 2001 and began studying the chemical elements and minerals on the Martian surface, looking for water below the surface, and measuring radiation around the planet.

Missions to Mars show how difficult space exploration can be and, in particular, what a challenge it is to send spacecraft to Mars. Several missions to the Red Planet have failed. The Soviet Union had trouble with every one of its Mars-bound probes—*Mars 2–7, Phobos 1–2,* and *Mars '96.* The United States experienced a huge loss when its *Mars Observer* craft, carrying many science instruments, vanished in space in 1993. To prepare for orbit, the craft turned off its transmitter while pressurizing its fuel tanks. Something went wrong, and the spacecraft was never recovered.

= PLANETARY EXPLORATION

After the success of *Mars Pathfinder*, NASA launched *Mars Climate Orbiter* in December 1998 and *Mars Polar Lander* in January 1999. As *Climate Orbiter* tried to orbit the planet, incorrect programming data caused it to get too low in the atmosphere. Months later, on December 3, 1999, planetary scientists and space enthusiasts waited anxiously as *Polar Lander* began its descent into the Martian atmosphere. Communication with the probe was not planned until it landed near the southern polar cap. But there was no communication, and no way to know what went wrong.

The Grand Tour: Exploring the Outer Planets

Jupiter and Saturn have mystified people for centuries. What is that Great Red Spot? Why does Saturn have rings? How many moons circle each planet? Astronomers thought they knew the answers, but the Pioneer and Voyager missions revealed those worlds to be stranger and more fascinating than expected.

Pioneer 10 was the first spacecraft to travel through the asteroid belt. Some scientists feared the craft might hit an asteroid, but it reached Jupiter safely in December 1973. *Pioneer 10* took the first up-close photographs of Jupiter, which showed the planet had colorful swirling bands. Photos revealed smaller white spots besides the Great Red Spot, which is a hurricane large enough to cover at least two Earths. The craft also measured Jupiter's strong magnetic field and radiation belts. *Pioneer 11* did the same, one year later.

Jupiter's Great Red Spot

Scientists did not have to wait long to see Jupiter and Saturn up close again. The United States launched two Voyager probes in 1977. *Voyager 1* quickly got to Jupiter, in March 1979. *Voyager 2* arrived four months later. Each probe photographed the planet and its four largest moons—Io, Europa, Ganymede, and Callisto—in more detail than ever before. Io has volcanoes and resembles a "pizza ball." Europa has a cracked, icy surface (and possibly a liquid ocean beneath the ice). The Voyager

---

While *Pioneer 10* headed into interstellar space (leaving the solar system in 1983), *Pioneer 11* flew by Saturn in 1979, the first probe to do so. It photographed and took measurements of the planet, its rings, and some of its moons, too. The spacecraft lost power in 1995.

PLANETARY EXPLORATION

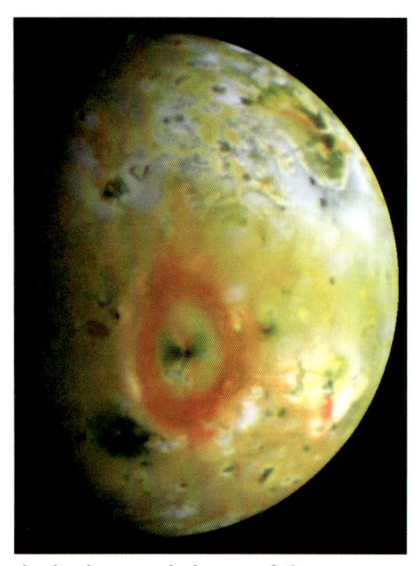

Jupiter's moon Io is one of the most volcanically active bodies in the solar system.

probes discovered that lightning crackles in Jupiter's cloud tops, a thin ring surrounds the planet, and Jupiter has many more moons than had been observed from Earth.

At Saturn in 1981, Voyager revealed the rings to be more complex and grand than expected. Dark spokes could be seen, and small moons were found that guided the ring material, like cowboys herding cattle. Saturn's largest moon, Titan, was also studied, though its atmosphere was too thick for Voyager's cameras to see the surface.

While *Voyager 1* headed out of the solar system, *Voyager 2* took advantage of a rare alignment of the outer planets. The spacecraft continued on to Uranus (1986) and then Neptune (1989), achieving the "Grand Tour." The craft detected faint rings around both gas giants and discovered new moons.

A spacecraft named *Galileo*, launched from the space shuttle in 1989, visited Jupiter in 1995 and stayed there. It released a small probe that plunged into Jupiter's cloud layers and measured temperature, pressure, chemical composition,

Cassini, launched in 1997, entered Saturn's orbit in July 2004. *Cassini* later released the European Space Agency's *Huygens* probe, which landed on Titan (Saturn's largest moon) in 2005.

Saturn and several of its moons, including Titan

52   SPACE EXPLORATION

= PLANETARY EXPLORATION

Earth

Uranus

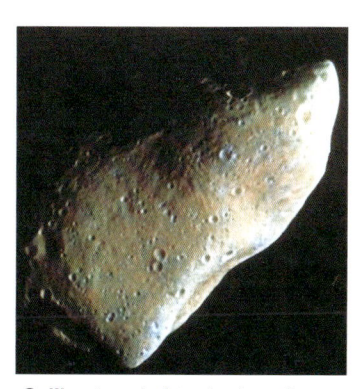

Galileo traveled to Jupiter via Venus and Earth, using the gravity of those planets to gain speed. It was the first probe to photograph an asteroid (Gaspra) up close. It also discovered a tiny moon named Dactyl orbiting the asteroid Ida, *above*.

and other characteristics before the planet's dense atmosphere crushed it. The orbiter flew around Jupiter often and visited the major moons, collecting much data. *Galileo* survived for eight years in the Jovian system despite the harsh radiation.

Wandering Through Space

Not every robot spacecraft visits a planet. Some head to much smaller objects—comets and asteroids. When world-famous Halley's Comet approached the Sun in 1986, some countries and space agencies launched probes to meet it. From the Soviet Union, two Vega spacecraft, which had visited Venus, flew by the comet first (in March 1986) and took measurements. A few days later, Japan's probe named *Sakigake* briefly passed by. Last and most daring was *Giotto*, a probe sent by the European Space Agency.

Giotto traveled into the fuzzy white "head" of Halley's Comet, a cloud of gas and dust surrounding the nucleus. More than 200 dust particles per second struck the craft. One dust grain (about a third of an ounce) knocked out communications with Earth for a short while, but the 9-foot-long cylinder-shaped probe survived its passage through the comet.

SPACE EXPLORATION 53

PLANETARY EXPLORATION

Giotto found that the nucleus of Halley's Comet was about 9 miles long and 6 miles wide. Although the comet lost about 35 tons of matter every hour as it neared the Sun, it still has enough material to survive a few hundred trips through the solar system.

Deep Space 1 was a spacecraft with no destination when it launched in October 1998. Its purpose was high-tech testing in outer space. The craft carried advanced technologies. Among the devices tested was an ion engine, first of its kind, that performed better and longer than expected. *Deep Space 1*'s mission was extended to encounter a near-Earth asteroid in 1999 and Comet Borrelly in 2001.

NASA launched *NEAR Shoemaker* in February 1996. The craft's name explained its objective: Near Earth Asteroid Rendezvous. It reached the small, potato-shaped asteroid Eros in February 2000. Not only was *NEAR Shoemaker* the first probe to orbit an asteroid, it also managed to land safely on the funny-looking rock.

> *NEAR Shoemaker* was named for Dr. Eugene Shoemaker, a famous geologist and astronomer who studied how asteroids and comets may have shaped the planets. He was co-discoverer of a comet (Shoemaker-Levy No. 9) that smashed spectacularly into Jupiter in 1994.

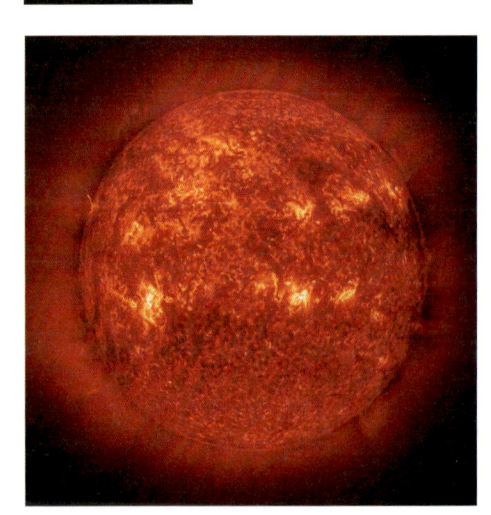

SOHO's view of the Sun in 2000

What About Our Sun?

Let's not forget the largest and most important member of the solar system. Several space probes have been sent into orbit to study our Sun. Some of the Pioneer series did so in the 1960s. Two Helios probes measured the solar wind in the mid-1970s. The Solar Maximum Mission observed solar flares in the 1980s. Then came *Ulysses* and *SOHO*.

Ulysses, launched in October 1990, was the first spacecraft to travel in an orbit nearly perpendicular (vertical) to the *ecliptic plane*. No human-made vehicle could produce the power to break

54 SPACE EXPLORATION

PLANETARY EXPLORATION

out of the ecliptic plane on its own, so *Ulysses* relied on mighty Jupiter's gravity to hurl it above that level. It was able to fly over the Sun's north and south poles, which had never been observed or measured in scientific detail before.

SOHO is the *So*lar and *H*eliospheric *O*bservatory. Launched in December 1995, *SOHO* was sent to study the nature of the Sun's *corona* and inner structure, as well as detect the *solar wind*. During its mission, *SOHO* discovered more than 50 sun-grazing comets and made movies of *coronal mass ejections,* which produce dangerous radiation that can cause communication blackouts on Earth.

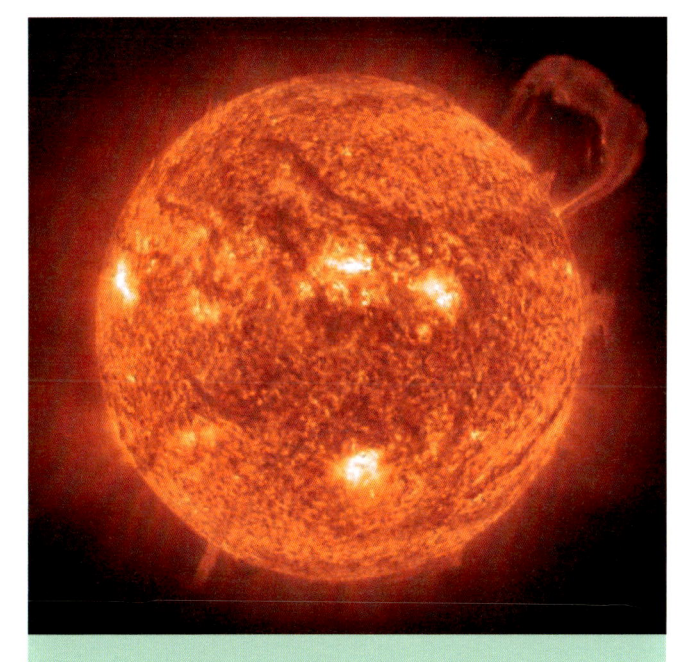

The **ecliptic plane** is a thin region of space around the Sun through which almost all the planets and other bodies of the solar system move during their orbits.

The **corona** is the outermost and thinnest part of the Sun's atmosphere. It is sometimes visible during a solar eclipse. The **solar wind** is a stream of charged particles coming from the corona.

SPACE EXPLORATION 55

International Space Station flight engineer Clay Anderson shows a microbial air sampler and petri dish in the Destiny laboratory.

Near-Earth Space Habitats

People need food, water, air, clothing, shelter, waste disposal, and some measure of safety to live. Earth gives us these things, but outer space does not (not even on other planets). There is no air to breathe in space. Space is either too cold or too hot for humans. Radiation from the Sun and cosmic rays can harm a person. There are small and large objects—natural (meteoroids) or artificial (pieces of rockets, paint chips, and other "space junk")—that travel fast enough to make holes in metal sheets or human skin.

A habitat built in space must provide everything essential for a comfortable life while shielding people from the dangers of space. There are four kinds of space habitats:

1. Spaceships (such as the space shuttle)
2. Space stations that orbit Earth (near-Earth habitats)
3. Bases and settlements on other worlds (such as the Moon and Mars)
4. Permanent structures in deep space

This section covers the space shuttle and space stations that go (or have gone) around Earth. The next section discusses the possibility of an inhabited base on the Moon or Mars. (The fourth kind of space habitat—deep-space structures—will not be discussed here.)

A spaceship is for travel; a space station is for living. A spaceship carries a person from one habitat (such as Earth) to another (the space station) and provides a comfortable environment for as long as the trip lasts. A space station, on the other hand, must keep people alive for months or years.

Features of a Near-Earth Habitat

Consumables are things that are used up and must continually be replaced. For a near-Earth space habitat, the consumables—food, clothing, water, and air (to start with)—are brought up from the ground.

On a large space station, water and air can be recycled and some food grown to reduce the amount that must be transported. Chemical "scrubbers" remove carbon dioxide and return clean air to the habitat. Water is recycled from the moisture collected from the air and from wastewater (including urine).

Many trips to a space station are necessary to bring enough supplies to keep the occupants alive and well for a long time. This is very expensive.

A space station keeps air at the same pressure as on the ground. This lets the occupants live and work in regular clothes rather than wear spacesuits all the time. The pressurized area also protects occupants from some levels of radiation and tiny meteoroids and space debris. To protect people from high radiation events, such as solar flares, a small heavily shielded area is usually provided.

For people to live in space for long periods, they must have a way to dispose of wastes—solid and liquid body wastes, wastewater from washing and cleaning, water from fuel cells that generate electricity, used food containers, packaging, and other trash. Water can be collected and recycled or discarded into space. Garbage usually is put into a robot craft that burns up in the atmosphere.

Heat is another waste product. People and equipment produce heat as they work. If there is no way to get rid of the excess heat, it will build up. Soon it would be too hot for either people or machines to work. This heat is collected from living and working areas and shed into space by radiators.

Fuel cells use hydrogen and oxygen to make electricity, also producing water. On the space shuttle, wastewater is dumped overboard, while water from fuel cells is saved and transferred to the International Space Station for drinking.

Sticking out into space, radiator panels work like the radiator in a car. A liquid passes through the hot area and absorbs heat. The hot fluid flows through the panels, where the heat is given off into space. This process cools the liquid, which is then pumped back to the hotter area to pick up more heat.

Salyut

The first space station to orbit Earth was named Salyut. The Soviet Union launched seven Salyuts between 1971 and 1982. The earliest Salyut stations were designed only for temporary operations. Crews flew to the stations in Soyuz spacecraft and were resupplied by unmanned Progress vehicles. *Salyut 6* (1977–82) and *Salyut 7* (1982–86) were designed for longer missions. The longest mission was 237 days. The last crew left *Salyut 7* in 1986. The space station re-entered Earth's atmosphere in 1991, burning up over Argentina.

Skylab

The United States launched its first space station, Skylab, in 1973 atop a Saturn V rocket, the same type that sent astronauts to the Moon. The third stage of the rocket was converted to provide living quarters, life support, and scientific instruments for a crew of three. Apollo command modules carried astronauts to and from Skylab.

Eleven days after Skylab was launched, three astronauts docked with it. They noticed one of two large solar panels had torn away. A second solar panel was jammed, and part of the heat shield was missing. The crew installed a cover over the

Skylab's orbit decayed faster than expected because greater than expected activity on the Sun "puffed up" the top of Earth's atmosphere, slowing the station down. Skylab was destroyed as it burned up in the atmosphere in 1979.

SPACE EXPLORATION

Three different crews lived on Skylab through 1974. They studied the properties of fluids and materials and the medical effects of microgravity (the nearly complete absence of gravity). They also observed the stars, the Sun, and Earth. Their missions proved people could live productively in space over long periods.

unshielded area to cool the spacecraft. They freed the jammed solar panel and restored power to the craft. These unplanned activities showed how people could repair equipment and structures in space.

Mir

In 1986, the Soviet Union launched the first module of Mir (meaning "peace"), the next generation of space stations. Unlike Salyut, the Mir space station could have modules attached to each other. Eventually, Mir grew to be a set of six modules that totaled 107 feet long and 90 feet wide.

Mir was occupied for more than 12 of its 15 years in orbit. It served as a home in space for 104 people representing 11 countries. One of the cosmonauts (Soviet/Russian astronauts), Dr. Valeri Polyakov, spent 438 days in space before returning to Earth. Three other cosmonauts spent at least one year in space.

The End of Mir. Mir had its share of problems. Once, the crew had to put out a dangerous fire. Another time, a resupply craft collided with the station, seriously damaging one module. Eventually, components designed to last three years began to fail. The space station was brought out of orbit in a controlled manner and crashed into the Pacific Ocean in 2001.

This photo of the space shuttle *Atlantis* docked with Mir was taken by the Mir-19 crew on July 4, 1995, as they undocked the *Soyuz* spacecraft from Mir for a brief fly-around.

The Space Shuttle

On March 12, 1981, a new era in space travel began. The space shuttle *Columbia* thundered off the launchpad at NASA's Kennedy Space Center in Florida. With astronauts John Young and Robert Crippen on board, the spaceship arched upward on a pillar of smoke and fire and disappeared into space.

Columbia was the first of a new kind of space vehicle. Previously, all rockets were expendable. After one flight, the entire rocket broke into pieces and fell into the ocean, went into orbit around the Sun, or burned up upon re-entry into the atmosphere. This was a waste of materials, effort, and money, since each space mission required a brand-new rocket. The space shuttle was built so that most of its parts could be used many times. Much of the space shuttle hardware has flown into space again and again.

The space shuttle, designed to provide frequent (every two to three weeks), low-cost flights to space, can do many tasks: lift heavy cargo (payloads) into space, carry laboratories where astronauts could conduct experiments; launch satellites, telescopes, and space probes; and bring components of a space station into orbit for assembly. A small habitat inside a shuttle could support seven people for up to 20 days in space.

> While the space shuttle was intended to be a method of transportation between the ground and low-Earth orbit, it became the only space habitat for astronauts from its first launch until the mid-1990s.

The space shuttle *Columbia* launches from Kennedy Space Center on March 12, 1981.

Components of the Shuttle

The space shuttle looks unlike any other rocket. At launch, it has three main components. The most important part is the delta-winged airplane-like vehicle called the orbiter—the only part that actually goes into orbit. The other main parts are a large, silo-like external tank and two solid rocket boosters. Standing on the launchpad, the shuttle looks as if it will never fly, but it is among the most powerful rockets ever built.

ORBITER

The orbiter looks like an airplane because it must fly as one for the return part of its flight. From nose to vertical tail, it is 122 feet long. Its wingspan is 78 feet. The crew's quarters are on two levels in the front, divided into a flight deck and a mid-deck.

The mission commander and pilot sit on the flight deck for the launch and re-entry. Their cockpit is similar to that of a commercial airliner, except the shuttle's cockpit has more computers and control sticks. Behind the commander and pilot, seats can be installed for two mission specialist astronauts who are trained to handle payloads and operate experiments.

The orbiter's mid-deck can have seats for four more astronauts. That brings the maximum crew size for a shuttle flight to eight. The walls of the mid-deck are lined with storage lockers for holding food supplies, tools, film, and equipment for experiments. Along one wall is a galley where meals can be prepared. Along another wall is a space toilet. An airlock from the mid-deck allows an astronaut to enter the payload bay, which is exposed to the vacuum of space.

Once the orbiter has reached orbit, large clamshell-like doors open along the orbiter's back to reveal a payload bay 60 feet long and 15 feet in diameter—large enough to hold one and one-half school buses. To

The Galileo spacecraft, carried aloft by the shuttle, weighed 2.5 tons. The shuttle can carry as much as 55,000 pounds of payload into an orbit about 100 miles high. The higher it goes, the less it can carry. At 320 miles above Earth, the shuttle's payload capacity drops to about 20,000 pounds.

assist the astronauts in handling payloads, a 50-foot-long robot arm is available, controlled from the aft flight deck.

The tail of the orbiter houses the three large rocket engines that are used during liftoff. Two smaller engines near the main are used to change the shuttle's orbit and start the orbiter on its return to Earth. Besides those five engines, 44 small thrusters are mounted in the nose and tail areas. The thrusters tilt and aim the orbiter while in space.

EXTERNAL TANK

The external tank holds the rocket fuel for the three main engines. Foam insulation keeps the super-cold liquid oxygen and liquid hydrogen inside at the proper temperatures. During a shuttle launch, the tank provides enough fuel to run the orbiter's main engines for approximately $8\frac{1}{2}$ minutes. The emptied tank is released and falls back to Earth, where it breaks apart over a remote ocean area. The external tank is the only part of the space shuttle that is discarded.

When it is time to sleep, an astronaut unpacks a sleeping bag, attaches it to a wall, and straps in securely. Anyone not strapped in would float away while sleeping.

> The space shuttle *Atlantis,* with its big external tank and two solid rocket boosters, is carried to the launchpad for another flight. The external tank is 154 feet long and 27.5 feet in diameter. Inside, the tank is divided into two smaller tanks, the upper of which holds more than 140,000 gallons of liquid oxygen. The lower tank holds more than 380,000 gallons of liquid hydrogen.

SOLID ROCKET BOOSTERS

When the shuttle takes off, most of its thrust comes from the two solid rocket boosters that are strapped to the sides of the external tank. Each booster is almost as tall as the external tank (149 feet long) but not half as thick (12.4 feet in diameter). Each carries more than one million pounds of solid fuel.

In flight, the two solid rocket boosters burn for slightly more than two minutes and lift the shuttle to 100,000 feet (about 20 miles). When the boosters run out of fuel, they separate from the external tank and drop into the ocean on parachutes.

NEAR-EARTH SPACE HABITATS

Shuttle Mission Profile

At 6.6 seconds before shuttle liftoff, the three main engines in the orbiter's tail begin firing. They take a few seconds to come up to full thrust. Hundreds of thousands of gallons of water drench the launchpad to muffle thunderous sound vibrations and reduce heat damage to launchpad equipment. Billowing white clouds leap outward and upward, and then the two solid rocket boosters ignite. Each booster comes up to full thrust in less than one second.

In a little more than two minutes of flight, with the orbiter's back leaning over the Atlantic Ocean, the two boosters run out of fuel. Explosive bolts separate the boosters from the external tank, and small thrusters in each booster's nose and tail push sideways to move the booster clear of the orbiter and tank. As the orbiter continues upward on the thrust of its three main engines, the boosters coast down toward the ocean. Parachutes slow their descent so the boosters are not damaged as they hit the water, where recovery ships retrieve them. Returned to shore, the boosters are cleaned and fueled for reuse.

A combined thrust of almost 7.8 million pounds starts the shuttle on its upward climb. Brilliant orange flames shoot out the back of the boosters and stretch downward for 600 to 700 feet—more than three times the length of the vehicle itself.

For $6\frac{1}{2}$ minutes after booster separation, the orbiter and external tank continue their upward climb until the external tank is empty. The main engines stop and the external tank is released. It falls to Earth and breaks up.

The orbiter's small engines complete the thrust to place the shuttle in orbit. Shortly after orbit is reached, the shuttle crew opens the payload bay doors. The orbiter rapidly builds up heat inside from its electronic equipment and the Sun's radiation. Radiators on the payload bay doors remove the excess heat.

When the mission is completed, the orbiter is prepared for return to Earth. It turns tail-first and, at the precise moment, the two small engines fire again, slowing the vehicle so it can begin its long fall to Earth.

About 400,000 feet up, the orbiter's underside, now facing downward, begins to feel the effects of atmospheric friction. The black underside glows as temperatures approach 2,000 degrees F. The underside is protected with thousands of tiles made of silica (silicon and oxygen compounds). The very hottest areas (front edge of the wing and on the orbiter's nose) are coated with dense carbon materials. The tiles and carbon materials protect the underside and keep it from burning away.

Eventually, the orbiter falls into air dense enough to let it fly as an airplane. Because the main engines have no fuel, the orbiter must glide to a runway at Kennedy Space Center or, if the weather is bad in Florida, at a location elsewhere in the country.

From the moment the orbiter touches down, launch crews begin preparations for its next mission in space. It is towed to a processing facility where new payloads are inserted. Next the orbiter goes to the Vehicle Assembly Building, where it is joined to a new external tank and two refueled boosters. In a few months, the orbiter is ready again for liftoff into space.

The astronauts typically spend five to 19 days doing the tasks needed to accomplish their mission. They also find time to relax, have fun, take pictures, admire the view of Earth, and talk to family, friends, and the public.

Near-Earth Space Habitats

Space Shuttle Payloads

The space shuttle can carry different kinds of payloads. The orbiter has carried satellites into space, and also scientific laboratories such as Spacelab (1983–97), built by the nations of the European Space Agency.

The shuttle has put large astronomical observatories into orbit. The Hubble Space Telescope went up in 1990, and the Chandra X-Ray Observatory in 1999. The shuttle also has launched robot spacecraft to other planets. That's how the *Magellan* probe got sent to Venus, and *Galileo* to Jupiter.

International Space Station

NASA began planning a permanent space station in the late 1960s. In 1984, President Ronald Reagan revealed the plans for Space Station Freedom, a cooperative effort among the United States, Canada, Japan, and some European countries. But the space station was redesigned yet again. In 1993 Russia and Brazil joined the project, and the name was changed to the International Space Station (ISS).

Fun Facts About the Space Shuttle

- In 8 1/2 minutes, the space shuttle accelerates at launch from zero to 17,400 miles per hour, almost nine times as fast as a rifle bullet.

- If the main engines pumped water instead of fuel, they would drain an average-sized swimming pool in 25 seconds.

- The solid rocket boosters consume more than 10 tons of fuel each second at launch.

- The orbiter has more than 2 1/2 million parts, including 230 miles of wire.

In the 1990s, the United States and Russia brought U.S. astronauts and Russian cosmonauts together to operate the Mir space station. Space shuttle *Atlantis* docked with Mir for the first time in 1995. It was one of nine trips to Mir to exchange crew members, bring supplies, and—in this case—deliver a new module to the station. The two countries gained valuable experience working together and laid the foundation for the eventual construction and operation of the International Space Station.

NEAR-EARTH SPACE HABITATS

The ISS is an engineering marvel, a challenge to design, construct, test, outfit, assemble, and operate, built to last 15 years. Sixteen countries are contributing to its construction. More than 100 major pieces are being or will be assembled in orbit more than 200 miles above Earth.

But why build another space station? Mir had gotten too old. The United States, Russia, and other countries wanted a larger, longer-lasting facility to do long-term research in space. The space shuttle had supported some research, but flights had been too few and too short. A bigger space station also would provide better research support services (such as data transmission) than the shuttle could ever provide.

> The space shuttle has flown, at most, nine flights in a year and usually just four to six flights. It has not yet achieved its goal of reducing the cost of getting into orbit. There have been fatal accidents and costly delays. The cost of operations is high because many people are needed to support the Space Transportation System, or STS, as NASA officially calls it. However, the shuttle currently is the only U.S. vehicle capable of manned spaceflight to low-Earth orbit. For now, it is the only way we can build the International Space Station.

> The 16 partner countries providing equipment and support for the International Space Station are the United States, Russia, Canada, Japan, Brazil, Belgium, Denmark, France, Germany, Italy, the Netherlands, Norway, Spain, Sweden, Switzerland, and the United Kingdom.

The million-pound ISS is the largest construction project ever attempted in space.

Purposes of the ISS

The International Space Station has several purposes. One of the most important is that the ISS provides a constant presence in space. Rather than spend a few weeks in space, astronauts and scientists can stay for three to six months to study the effects of weightlessness on the human body and to do experiments in microgravity.

SPACE EXPLORATION 67

The research done aboard the ISS may lead to breakthroughs in medicine, engineering, and technology that will have practical uses for humanity. The research could create jobs and economic opportunities tomorrow and in the decades to come. As an investment in the future, the ISS provides ways to do research that cannot be done on Earth.

The ISS shows how countries can work together for the peaceful use of space. We can accomplish greater feats (like a manned mission to Mars) with cooperation rather than competition. Also, the lessons we learn from building and operating the ISS will prepare us for future manned missions in space exploration.

Components of the ISS

The International Space Station is made of cylinder-shaped modules and other large parts that are built on the ground, then assembled and maintained in space. The station can be expanded if desired in the future.

- The first piece, a control module named Zarya ("Sunrise"), came from Russia and was put into orbit by a Russian rocket in November 1998. Zarya has docking ports for additional modules and solar arrays for power.
- The second piece was Unity, which a space shuttle carried into orbit in December 1998. As its name suggests, Unity is a small module that allows six other modules to be connected together.
- The ISS became a working space habitat when the third piece, the service module Zvezda ("Star") from Russia, was attached to the station in July 2000. Zvezda provided living quarters and life-support systems for the first few crews.
- Destiny, a U.S. laboratory, was delivered in February 2001. Scientific research aboard the station could now begin.

More components have been added since. The central girder or truss, which is a set of long beams fitted together, connects the modules and the main solar power arrays. The truss provides a rigid framework for the station.

NEAR-EARTH SPACE HABITATS

Canada's Space Station Remote Manipulator System can creep slowly along the outside of the space station like an inchworm.

Various countries are providing other pieces of the ISS. The Space Station Remote Manipulator System, provided by Canada, is a 58-foot-long robot arm that helps with assembly and maintenance. The arm travels along the truss on a moving platform. Four solar arrays, which provide electrical power, rotate on the truss to stay facing the Sun. Six large radiators provide cooling in pressurized areas. From Italy and Brazil have come cargo containers. The Quest airlock, from the United States, allows crew members to conduct spacewalks without the space shuttle being present.

An emergency crew return vehicle (at first, a Soyuz spacecraft) is always docked at the ISS while it is inhabited. This assures the safe return of all crew members if a hazardous situation (such as a fire) occurs on the space station and a quick departure must be made.

> An **airlock** is a small room with one door to the pressurized area and another door to the outside (space). A control panel allows a crew member to release the air out to space, after which the door to the outside can be opened. Another control pumps air back into the airlock until the pressure is equal with the interior of the space station.

SPACE EXPLORATION 69

Near-Earth Space Habitats

Without gravity, hot air does not rise. Aboard the ISS, an oven has a fan that forces the hot air to move around. Hot metal shelves conduct heat directly to food containers.

Living and Working in Microgravity

It isn't easy to provide for eating, drinking, sleeping, cleaning, and personal hygiene on the space station. Air, water, materials, and the human body act differently in space because of microgravity. Equipment we use on Earth would not work the same way, or not work at all, aboard the space station.

Food for ISS crews is nutritious and compact, and tasty most of the time. The food must come in convenient packages for easy handling in weightlessness. Astronauts select their menus before going to the space station, but their choices are limited. Fresh foods are sometimes available, although they do not last long. Water must be added to most items to make them edible.

The ISS is designed to be maintained while in orbit. Most parts, inside or outside, can be disconnected, replaced, and reconnected (like a light bulb). This makes it easier for the crew to make repairs.

> When completed, the ISS will fly over 85 percent of Earth's surface and 95 percent of Earth's population and will be as bright as Venus.

Personal hygiene is a novel experience on the ISS. A crew member takes a shower using a hand sprayer. Because water droplets float around in weightlessness (which could be a hazard for electrical equipment), the bather must catch the sprayed water in a sponge or washcloth. In space, toothpaste is swallowed. Shampoo is rubbed into the hair and dried with a towel without rinsing. A razor (using a vacuum tube) sucks the cut hair off an astronaut's face.

At intervals, Russia launches a Progress resupply rocket stocked with food, water, personal items, and spare parts. The Progress spacecraft attaches to a Russian-made module. The crew uses supplies from Progress and fills the craft with trash. Eventually, the Progress undocks from the station and burns up in the atmosphere, incinerating the trash it carries.

NEAR-EARTH SPACE HABITATS

The European Space Agency and Japan have built reusable modules that fit in the space shuttle's payload bay. The modules may be unloaded while the shuttle is docked or left attached to the station for longer use. Eventually, the reusable modules travel back to Earth for refilling.

Crew members can work outside for about eight hours at a time—wearing spacesuits, of

Crew members wear small gas jetpacks that can get them back to the station if they get separated from the spacecraft.

Space-shuttle crews wear spacesuits made with 14 layers of fabric. Going from the inside out, there's nylon tricot, spandex, a lacing of plastic tubes, urethane-coated nylon, polyester fiber, ripstop nylon, seven layers of polyester film, and an outer layer made of fibers that are lighter and tougher than steel.

Those same stronger-than-steel fibers, called *aramid* fibers, are used to make bulletproof vests for police officers and flameproof suits for firefighters. One of the best-known aramids has the trade name Kevlar.

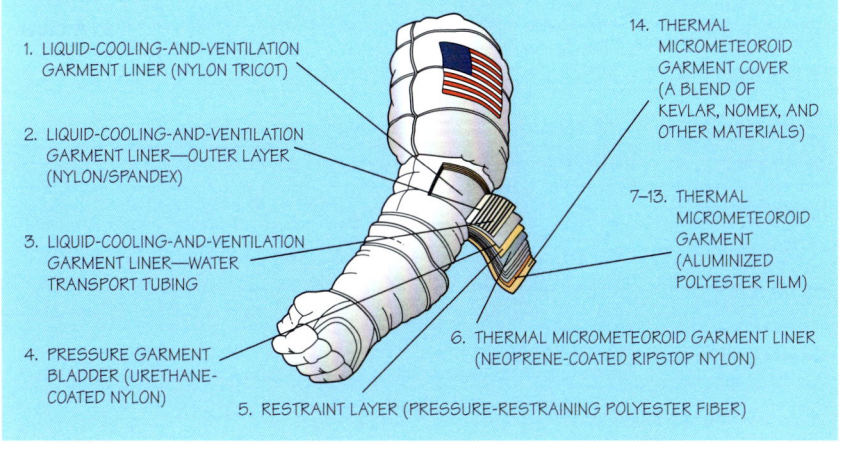

1. LIQUID-COOLING-AND-VENTILATION GARMENT LINER (NYLON TRICOT)
2. LIQUID-COOLING-AND-VENTILATION GARMENT LINER—OUTER LAYER (NYLON/SPANDEX)
3. LIQUID-COOLING-AND-VENTILATION GARMENT LINER—WATER TRANSPORT TUBING
4. PRESSURE GARMENT BLADDER (URETHANE-COATED NYLON)
5. RESTRAINT LAYER (PRESSURE-RESTRAINING POLYESTER FIBER)
6. THERMAL MICROMETEOROID GARMENT LINER (NEOPRENE-COATED RIPSTOP NYLON)
7–13. THERMAL MICROMETEOROID GARMENT (ALUMINIZED POLYESTER FILM)
14. THERMAL MICROMETEOROID GARMENT COVER (A BLEND OF KEVLAR, NOMEX, AND OTHER MATERIALS)

SPACE EXPLORATION

course. While they work in space, they have several ways to move around. They can pull themselves hand-over-hand using handholds on the modules. They can ride on a small railcar along the truss of the station. Or they can hitch a ride on a robot arm. Crew members use tether lines to stay attached to the ISS, keeping them from drifting away if they lose their grip.

ISS Crews

The ISS can hold a crew of three to seven people (a group called an expedition) for up to six months. Crew members arrive and depart in either a space shuttle or a Soyuz spacecraft. Most occupants have been American astronauts or Russian cosmonauts. A few wealthy "tourists" have paid for a few days' visit. The official language is English, but a lot of Russian gets spoken, too.

> The first crew, known as Expedition One, boarded the station in November 2000. American Commander Bill Shepherd and Russians Yuri Gidzenko and Sergei Krikalev stayed for four months. They were replaced by Expedition Two, which had a Russian commander and two Americans, including the first woman on the station, Susan Helms.

When the ISS is complete, it will be 365 feet wide, 290 feet deep, and 100 feet tall—about as big inside as the passenger cabins of two 747 jets.

Most crews have a commander, a flight engineer, and a science officer. The commander has the overall responsibility for running the station and managing the crew. The engineer's main duty is to keep the station's mechanical and electrical systems working properly. The science officer supervises the scientific and medical experiments. Additional crew members will work mainly on science experiments. All of the crew take part in medical experiments and station maintenance.

Science on the ISS

The ISS may have as many as seven laboratory modules, becoming four times larger and having more research abilities than any previous space station. The United States will provide a supporting laboratory besides Destiny. Three research modules will come from Russia and one each from Japan and the European Space Agency. In addition, the Brazilian Express Pallet will hold experiments that need to be outside on the truss.

Some experiments done aboard the ISS study the effects of microgravity on the human body and on other creatures. Some investigate various properties of physics and chemistry. Some may produce new materials that cannot be made on Earth.

Medical research aboard the ISS may lead to the development of drugs that can stop bone loss. Besides helping space travelers, such drugs would benefit millions of older people. Other studies in space might lead to a treatment for cancer or find ways to make purer forms of medicines. Other research might explain how plants and animals could behave at different levels of gravity, such as one-sixth Earth's gravity (as on the Moon) or one-third (as on Mars).

Scientists want to better understand how physical laws and chemical processes work in space. Materials act differently, fluids flow differently, and fire burns differently in a microgravity environment. New materials could be made in orbit from substances that will not stay mixed on Earth due to their different densities. (See "All Mixed Up.") Studies of the process of burning could lead to improvements in firefighting techniques and equipment, or help to strengthen pollution controls.

The knowledge gained from experiments that are not possible on Earth will benefit us all. The International Space Station is the next step to satisfy humanity's ancient yearning to explore, learn, and achieve. From this outpost, we can continue to explore the frontier of space.

This photograph by cosmonaut Nikolai Budarin of the ISS Expedition Six shows how strange space gardening can be. The air bubble trapped in this water drop doesn't rise because in space there is no buoyancy. The droplet rests on the leaf without bending the stalk or falling off because of zero-gravity.

Flames in microgravity look different from those we see. On Earth, a flame is shaped like a teardrop and yellow in color. On the ISS, it would be round and blue.

> **All Mixed Up.** Imagine you are trying to mix molten lead and molten aluminum. The large difference in densities will cause them to separate in Earth's gravity before the metals can cool into solid metal. In weightlessness, however, the two could mix to form a new material (an *alloy*). Perhaps a new material that was similarly made could be used to build future spacecraft.

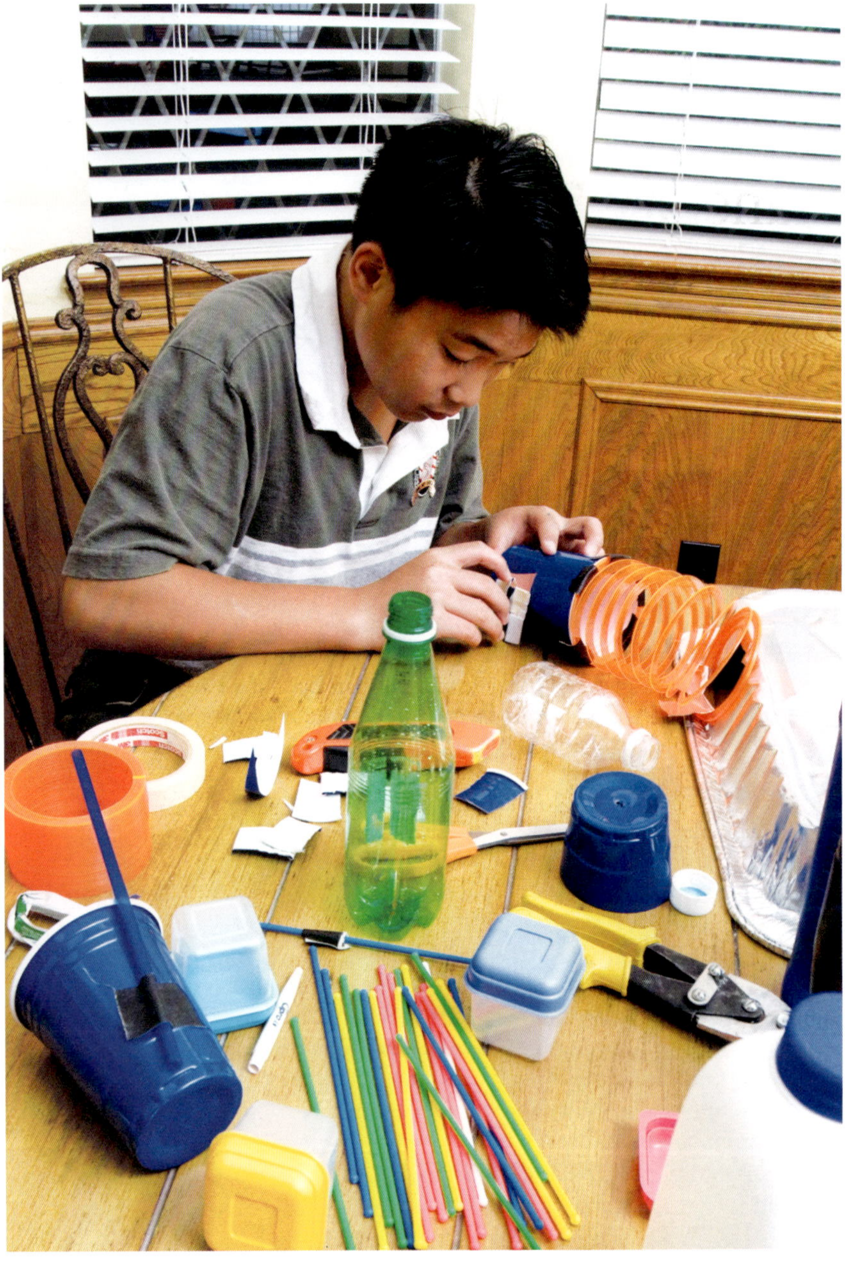

Planetary Bases and Settlements in Space

Where would we build space bases and settlements? The Moon and Mars are current candidates. Bases and settlements could also be built on asteroids, on the moons of other planets, and even in space itself. At first, these bases will depend on supplies from Earth, but they could eventually become self-sufficient.

Moon Bases

The Moon is just a few days of travel from Earth. Earth-Moon communication takes only a few seconds round-trip. We have had experience with manned operations on the Moon. The gravity is only one-sixth of Earth's, so landing on and lifting off from the Moon's surface does not take much fuel. All of these are advantages.

There are also disadvantages of establishing a lunar base. The Moon does not have an atmosphere. On its surface, people would be unprotected from space radiation and the impacts of micrometeorites. The Moon rotates about once a month, creating a scorching hot day (+250 degrees F) that lasts two weeks, followed by an intensely cold night (-250 degrees F) that also lasts two weeks. No one knows how the low gravity might affect the growth of children or the aging process.

For these reasons, the Moon is not the best place to start a colony. But it is suitable for scientific research and mining operations.

Purposes of a Moon Base

A moon base would allow continued exploration of the Moon. We can search for valuable materials, such as water ice below the surface. Bases near the north or south poles would receive sunlight almost all the time. Explorers working out of those bases might find polar ice deposits in nearby areas that are always in darkness.

We also might set up an astronomical observatory. A telescope on the Moon's stable surface, looking out through no air, would have a superb view of the universe. A base on the far side of the Moon would be valuable for radio astronomy, since it would be shielded from almost all the radio "noise" generated on Earth.

Businesses might be able to mine lunar material for a profit. Metals could be smelted from moon rocks to make building materials and solar cells. Oxygen, taken out of the rocks, would provide breathable air. Someday a lunar hotel or resort could be built, followed by a lunar colony.

Living on the Moon

A moon base would have modules for laboratories and living quarters. The modules would be buried, except for their entrances, to shield the inhabitants from radiation. The lunar soil would also insulate the base from extreme temperatures.

The modules would have the same life-support functions as a space station, providing a breathable atmosphere, clean water, food, power, and temperature control. Water would be recycled as much as possible. Most food would be imported from Earth. A crew would either stay at the base or visit regularly to maintain and repair equipment and do scientific work.

At first, all of the modules would be built on Earth and hauled to the Moon. Since this will be expensive, a moon base will grow faster if lunar materials are used to build the modules. Once we develop the technology to mine, process, and transport lunar ore, a settlement on the Moon will be highly desirable.

Mars Bases

Mars has many advantages for a base or settlement. The planet has an atmosphere (almost all carbon dioxide) that would protect anyone on the surface from micrometeorites and partly from space radiation. The atmosphere is thick enough to produce wind and clouds, and maybe support an airplane. However, the air has no oxygen and there is not enough air pressure for a person to survive. Anyone exploring the surface of Mars will need to wear a spacesuit, just like on the Moon.

The gravity on Mars is about 40 percent as strong as Earth's, so humans and animals might be able to grow and reproduce there normally. A day on Mars is only slightly longer than on Earth, so a person could easily adapt to a Martian day.

Mars has huge quantities of ice buried under the surface in many places, and on the surface in the polar areas. There may be salty water under the ice, which could be tapped by drilling. Elements, such as sodium and chlorine, dissolved in the salty water could be separated and used. Mars rocks would also contain useful metals. In fact, most of the materials we would need to build a base or colony probably exist on Mars. And rocket propellants can be made using the carbon dioxide atmosphere and water on Mars. This can greatly reduce the cost of missions to Mars and Mars settlements.

But Mars has its disadvantages, too. The planet is much farther away than the Moon. With current technology, it would take between five and six months for a crew to reach Mars' orbit from the Earth. With better technology, using nuclear-powered ion rockets, the trip might be cut to two months. Cargo-only vehicles could be sent as "slow boats" to use less energy, taking as long as a year to reach Mars. Any crew that takes a trip to Mars would have to stay there for about two years.

> Because Mars is far from the Sun, it does not get hot. However, it can get cold enough in winter for dry ice to form directly from the carbon dioxide in the atmosphere.

Building a Mars Base

Before starting to build a base on Mars, we will need to send robot rovers to locate several promising sites. Then humans will survey those sites to find the best location for building the first base.

What would be a good place for a base? We would like a location near the equator for warmth, if possible. But we would also want a site with access to ice or water, and that might be closer to the poles. The kinds of resources available in the rocks nearby would be important. If we could use the water on Mars, we would not need to bring it from Earth, making it much cheaper to build and maintain a base.

A low-lying location would provide the best protection from space radiation. However, just as on the Moon, all permanent habitats would be buried underground, to reduce radiation exposure. (Temporary habitats could be on the surface, but they would have to withstand the raging dust storms on Mars.)

Just like on the Moon, the first parts to build the base would come from Earth. Bulldozers and backhoes could be used to dig holes and bury the habitat modules. To dig for water or to look for life, heavy drilling equipment would be designed to operate under Mars conditions. All habitat modules would be insulated against the cold.

The base would need energy for heat and to run its equipment. Some power could come from solar panels during the day, but a small nuclear reactor would be ideal for power around the clock. Electricity from the reactor could be used to turn carbon dioxide (from the air) and water or ice (from the crust) into oxygen, hydrogen, and other materials. The oxygen could be used directly to make breathable air. It might also be possible to ship a small smelter and manufacturing plant to Mars, for turning local materials into metal and parts for new habitat modules. The water found there might make it possible to use other kinds of construction materials, such as locally produced concrete.

Living on Mars

The oxygen and hydrogen from Mars' water could be used as rocket propellants and to power "over-the-road" vehicles. Vehicles for traveling on the surface of Mars could include rovers large enough for several people, and buggies that

PLANETARY BASES AND SETTLEMENTS IN SPACE

space-suited crew members could ride. The crew would stay busy maintaining the base, conducting research and prospecting for better supplies of water and minerals. They would explore and learn about the topography, geology, and weather of Mars.

Food for the crew would come from Earth at first. But eventually food could be grown locally. Mars has enough sunlight for plants to grow in pressurized greenhouses, but keeping them warm would take much energy. By the time we are ready to go to Mars, we may know how to make some food synthetically, without using plants at all.

Build a Space Habitat

For requirement 7, you are to design a space habitat. You can find material for this project around the house and in your family's recycling bin. A little thought and ingenuity can make a potato-chip tube into a lunar rover. Soda straws become the axles; bottle caps become the wheels. Aluminum foil can be wrapped around the tube, and a glue gun helps put it all together. A three-liter soda bottle and similar imagination can make a habitation module, a colony, or a space base. A cereal box can become a hangar bay for ground and space operations.

As you plan this project, ask yourself: What is the base's intended use? How have you provided for crew quarters, power, breathable air, radiation protection, food, water, and transportation? Your design must satisfy all these needs.

SPACE EXPLORATION 79

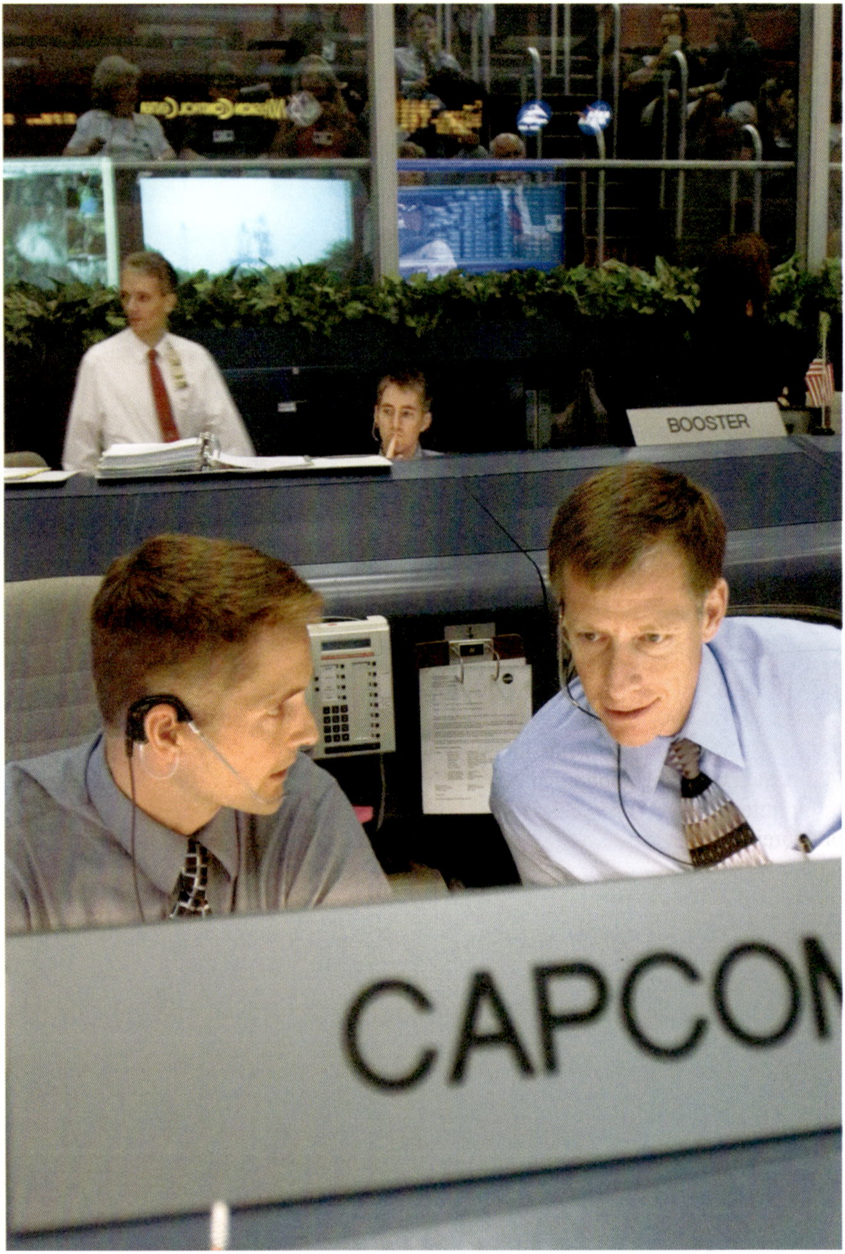
BOOSTER
CAPCOM

Careers in Space Exploration

A career in space exploration makes you think of being an astronaut. Since 64 percent of the present and former astronauts were Boy Scouts, you have a good head start. But astronautics is only one occupation among the many that will be needed to explore and settle our solar system and beyond. Many positions at NASA, at educational facilities, and in private businesses involve space exploration and research.

Getting Ready

To prepare for a space career, you must study math and science. Take all the high-school math you can—algebra, geometry, trigonometry, and calculus. Also take biology, chemistry, physics, and computer science.

You must be able to write and speak clearly. Being bilingual and having good people skills are vital in this age of the International Space Station. Study English and at least one foreign language. You will also need social studies including history, geography, international studies, art, drama, and music. All of these will widen your world and make you a better communicator.

To get into college, you will need good grades and high scores on standard exams such as the SAT (Scholastic Aptitude Test) or ACT (American College Test). In college, choose a technical or science major—physics, chemistry, biology, geology, mathematics, engineering, computer science, or premedicine. Round out your education with humanities courses such as languages, history, economics, art, and public speaking.

> The Mercury, Gemini, and Apollo programs in the 1960s harnessed the talents of more than 250,000 employees at NASA, universities, and various companies.

If you want to be a pilot astronaut, a military background is helpful. If you want to be a mission specialist astronaut, a scientific or medical background is helpful. Most importantly, follow the path where your interests lie.

Where Is the Work?

Other than at NASA, you might work at a university as a principal investigator for an experiment on the International Space Station. You might be a science teacher or someone who trains the astronauts. You might be a medical researcher who studies the effects of spaceflight, or a doctor who keeps the astronauts healthy. You might work at a university on a grant from NASA's Astrobiology Institute to search for life on Mars or under Europa's icy surface.

> You might provide independent services to NASA, as Mike Malin did. He developed the camera on the *Mars Global Surveyor,* which has given us the best map, to date, of the surface features on Mars.

Also, small private companies are developing new technologies for spaceflight. Some strive to build rockets that will send tourists into space at affordable prices. You might decide to work for a company that is building a spacecraft to fly to another planet. Or you might form your own business to provide access to space for your own reasons. To do any of these occupations, you will need a college degree in engineering or business, or both.

A Sampling of Careers

Requirement 8 asks you to find out the qualifications, education, and preparation required for two possible space careers, and to discuss the major responsibilities of those positions. Here's a closer look at some space careers, and a list of careers you might explore on your own.

Aerospace engineering and operations technicians work with systems used to test, launch, or track aircraft and space vehicles. Like all engineering technicians, those who specialize in aerospace apply science, math, and engineering principles to solve technical problems. They may assist engineers and scientists with research, by building or setting up equipment, preparing and conducting experiments, collecting data, and calculating the results. Engineering technicians need creativity to help with design work, often using computer-aided design (CAD) software or making prototypes of newly designed equipment. They must be able to work with their hands to build and repair small, detailed items without making errors.

Most positions for engineering technicians require at least a two-year associate degree in engineering technology. Training is available at technical institutes, community colleges, and vocational-technical schools and in the Armed Forces. Engineering technicians often work as part of a team of engineers and other specialists.

Aerospace engineers design, develop, and test aircraft, spacecraft, and missiles. They develop new technologies for space exploration, often specializing in areas such as structural design, propulsion systems, navigation and control, instrumentation, and communications. Aerospace engineers who work with spacecraft are also called astronautical engineers.

A bachelor's degree in engineering is required for almost all entry-level engineering positions. Most engineers earn their degrees in electrical, electronics, mechanical, or civil engineering. Many aerospace engineers are trained in mechanical engineering. Engineering students typically spend their first two years of college studying math, basic sciences, introductory engineering, humanities, and social sciences. Courses in their last two years are mostly in engineering, usually concentrating in one branch. The last two years of an aerospace program might include courses in fluid mechanics, heat transfer, applied aerodynamics, flight vehicle design, trajectory dynamics, and aerospace propulsion systems.

No matter what your specialty, you must be able to communicate and work well with others as part of a team. You must be good at solving problems.

Research associates may take part in experiments or help analyze data for research projects such as mapping the planets and their moons. This work generally requires a master's degree, which takes two to three years of study beyond a bachelor's degree.

Space scientists must have at least a Ph.D. degree, which usually takes four to six years of study beyond a bachelor's degree. Scientists work with existing projects and are also expected to use their creativity to develop future missions. Space scientists need a broad base of knowledge. A scientist whose major field is chemistry, for instance, also needs a good grounding in physics, mathematics, and engineering.

Consider these careers:

- A **systems programmer** who designs, writes, and maintains computer programs for scientific analysis or for controlling a telescope in space

- A **systems analyst** who improves the performance of complex systems, such as making it easier for astronauts to conduct experiments aboard a space station

- An **engineer** in the areas of automation and robotics, materials and structures, propulsion and power systems, flight systems, measurement and instrumentation systems, data systems, experimental facilities and equipment

- A **space scientist** specializing in meteorology, ionospherics, lunar and planetary studies, radiation fields and particles, meteoroid studies

- A **life scientist** specializing in psychology, physiology, microbiology, hematology, neurobiology, botany, exobiology, biochemistry, interactions between human and machine systems

CAREERS IN SPACE EXPLORATION

In the future, space-related careers will be varied and indescribable in today's terms. Some occupations could take you into space; others could help someone else get there. We stand on the shore of a great sea and can only imagine what lies beyond the horizon. Perhaps your career will allow you to find out!

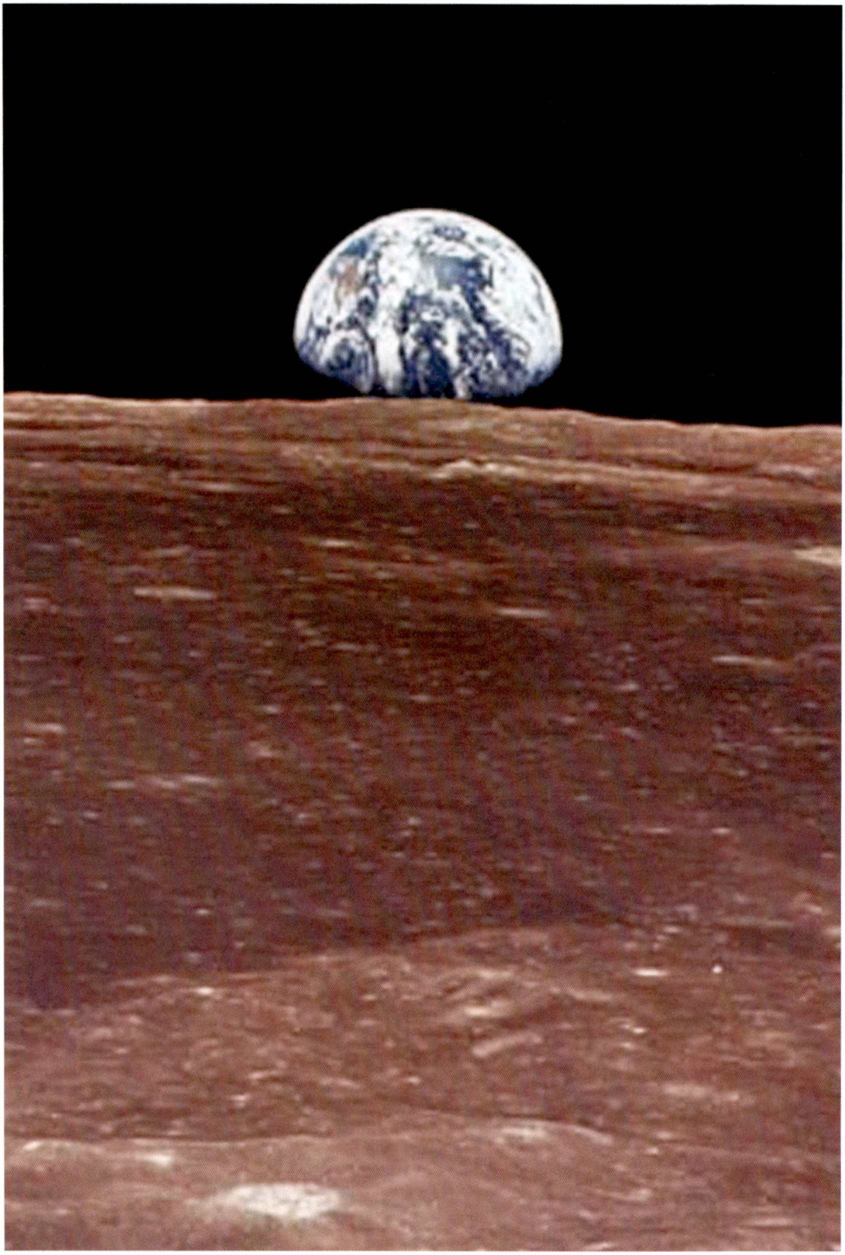

The Greatest Adventure

Earlier we asked: Why explore space? We have covered several possible answers to that question, but they can all be summed up like this: Because it is human to do so. People have always explored the environment around them. As we have observed, experimented, and taken risks, we have learned how to better protect and maintain our environment and improve our way of life.

> Exploring space helps us better understand and protect our home planet. As we begin our move into the universe, we look back at our home world and see how small, yet how beautiful, it is. Boundaries of states and nations are invisible. It becomes obvious that Earth itself is a great spaceship on an unending journey and that all of us are astronauts. Space exploration is the greatest adventure of all.

Space Exploration Resources

Information about space exploration changes constantly. Each new mission makes discoveries and shows that some of our old ideas were incorrect. When you look up information about space and humankind's efforts to explore it, always try to find a recently published book or a dependable website. Books that are only two years old may contain some obsolete information. Not all websites are updated frequently or accurately. Look for the best and most current information available.

Scouting Literature

Astronomy, Atomic Energy, Aviation, Chemistry, Computers, Electricity, Electronics, Engineering, Geology, Inventing, Photography, Radio, and *Robotics* merit badge pamphlets

Visit the Boy Scouts of America's official retail website at http://www.scoutstuff.org for a complete listing of all merit badge pamphlets and other helpful Scouting materials and supplies.

Books

Berger, Melvin, et al. *Can You Hear a Shout in Space? Questions and Answers About Space Exploration.* Econo-Clad Books, 2001.

Chaikin, Andrew, and James A. Lovell. *Space.* Carlton, 2002.

Dethloff, Henry C., and Ronald A. Schorn. *Voyager's Grand Tour: To the Outer Planets and Beyond.* Smithsonian Press, 2003.

Dyson, Marianne J. *Home on the Moon: Living on a Space Frontier.* National Geographic, 2003.

———. *Space Station Science: Life in Free Fall.* Scholastic, 1999.

Engelhardt, Wolfgang. *The International Space Station: A Journey Into Space.* Tessloff/BSV Publishing USA, 1998.

Furniss, Tim. *The Atlas of Space Exploration.* Sterling, 2001.

Lee, Wayne. *To Rise From Earth: An Easy-to-Understand Guide to Spaceflight.* Second edition. Facts on File, 1999.

Mullane, R. Mike. *Do Your Ears Pop in Space? And 500 Other Surprising Questions About Space Travel.* John Wiley & Sons, 1997.

Reich, Tony, editor. *Space Shuttle: The First 20 Years—the Astronauts' Experiences in Their Own Words.* DK Publishing, 2002.

Sagan, Carl, and Carol Sagan. *Pale Blue Dot.* Random House, 1997.

Voigt, Gregory, and Alwyn T. Cohall. *Space Exploration Projects for Young Scientists.* Scholastic, 1995.

Voit, Mark. *Hubble Space Telescope: New Views of the Universe.* Harry N. Abrams, 2000.

Organizations and Websites

American Institute of Aeronautics and Astronautics
1801 Alexander Bell Drive, Suite 500
Reston, VA 20191-4344
Telephone: 703-264-7500
Website: http://www.aiaa.org

European Space Agency
Website: http://www.esa.int

The ESA calls itself "Europe's gateway to space." It has 17 member countries, including France, Germany, and the United Kingdom.

Galileo 1/45 Scale Model
Website: http://www.jpl.nasa.gov/galileo/model.html

This website describes *Galileo* as "one of the most complex robotic spacecraft ever flown." Visit the website for plans to build a detailed scale model of *Galileo*.

Goddard Space Flight Center
Website: http://www.gsfc.nasa.gov

The Center is "home to the nation's largest organization of combined scientists and engineers dedicated to learning and sharing their knowledge of the sun, Earth, solar system, and universe.

Great Images in NASA
Website: http://grin.hq.nasa.gov

GRIN boasts a collection of more than a thousand images "of significant historical interest" available for public viewing.

Jet Propulsion Laboratory
4800 Oak Grove Drive
Pasadena, CA 91109
Telephone: 818-354-4321
Website: http://www.jpl.nasa.gov

The JPL is considered NASA's leading "center for robotic exploration of the solar system."

Johnson Space Center
Space Center Houston
1601 NASA Road 1
Houston, TX 77058
Telephone: 281-244-2100
JSC website: http://www.nasa.gov/centers/johnson/home/index.html
Website about opportunities at NASA:
http://www.nasa.gov/about/career/index.html
SCH website:
http://www.spacecenter.org

Space Center Houston is the Johnson Space Center's official visitor center.

Junior Engineering Technical Society
1420 King Street, Suite 405
Alexandria, VA 22314
Telephone: 703-548-5387
Website: http://www.jets.org

JETS promotes interest in engineering, mathematics, and technology among high school students and gives them real-world engineering and problem-solving experiences.

Kennedy Space Center
Telephone: 321-449-4444
Website: http://www.nasa.gov/centers/kennedy/home/index.html

The Center is dedicated to "telling the story of how the United States built a space program that launched men to the Moon, orbited satellites that have improved our lives, and sent probes into distant space . . . ."

Marshall Space Flight Center
Website: http://www.nasa.gov/centers/marshall/home/index.html

Part of the Marshall Space Flight Center's mission is "bringing people to space; bringing space to people."

National Aeronautics and Space Administration
Telephone: 202-358-0001
Website: http://www.nasa.gov

NASA's website has a bounty of information about space exploration for students of all ages.

National Association of Rocketry
P.O. Box 407
Marion, IA 52302
Toll-free telephone: 800-262-4872
Website: http://www.nar.org

The NAR is the world's oldest and largest sport rocketry organization. Visit the website to find the club nearest you.

National Space Society
1620 I St. NW, Suite 615
Washington, DC 20006
Telephone: 202-429-1600
Website: http://www.nss.org

Planetary Society
65 North Catalina Ave.
Pasadena, CA 91106-2301
Telephone: 626-793-5100
Website: http://www.planetary.org

Smithsonian National Air and Space Museum
Sixth and Independence Ave., SW
Washington, DC 20560
Telephone: 202-633-1000
Website: http://www.nasm.si.edu

Part of the Smithsonian Institution, the museum maintains the world's largest collection of historic air and spacecraft.

Acknowledgments

The Boy Scouts of America thanks the National Space Society of North Texas and the Austin (Texas) Space Frontier Society for their hard work and diligence in updating the *Space Exploration* merit badge pamphlet and preparing the new manuscript. The following individuals in particular should be credited for their major contributions.

- **Louis Mazza,** a longtime space advocate and historian. Mr. Mazza served as chair of the editing committee formed to update the pamphlet and also was the primary writer for the space history section. He coordinated the entire project very effectively.

- **Curtis Kling,** a software systems engineer. Mr. Kling is the club's newsletter editor. He wrote the section on the unmanned planetary mission, helped polish the manuscript, and performed a final edit of the manuscript before submission.

- **Abigail Plemmons,** a doctoral candidate in Space Science at the University of Texas at Dallas. A real-life space scientist, Ms. Plemmons contributed to the chapter called "The Way Things Work."

- **Mark Plemmons,** a physicist in the semiconductor business. Mr. Plemmons contributed to the chapter called "The Way Things Work."

- **Tracy Benninger,** physicist and graduate of the University of Texas at Dallas in space science. Ms. Benninger is the Webmaster for the NSS of North Texas. She contributed to the chapter called "The Way Things Work."

- **Carol Johnson,** physicist, space advocate, and aerospace systems engineer. Ms. Johnson worked on the Heat Rejection Subsystem radiators for the International Space Station; the hardware she helped build is now in orbit. She wrote the sections about the space shuttle and the ISS, and contributed to the overall editing and reviewing of the manuscript.

- **Terry O'Hanlon,** an electrical technician for Raytheon and a space advocacy writer. Mr. O'Hanlon focused his energies on the chapter called "Careers in Space Exploration."

- **John Strickland Jr.,** senior analyst III for the Texas Department of Transportation (Information Systems Division). Mr. Strickland serves as coordinator for the Robert A. Heinlein and Wernher von Braun awards for the NSS. He wrote the sections about space habitats on the Moon and Mars and also contributed to the section on why we explore space.

The National Space Society of North Texas and the Austin Space Frontier Society are chapters of the National Space Society, a nonprofit, international, educational organization dedicated to the creation of a free spacefaring civilization. It was created in 1986 by the merger of the National Space Institute, which was founded in 1974 by Dr. Wernher von Braun, and Keith Henson's L5 Society.

Photo and Illustration Credits

Jonathan N. Harris, Space Debris Inc., www.space-debris.com, courtesy—page 15

©2008 Jupiter Images—cover *(astronaut, Mars)*

Louis Mazza, courtesy—page 40

NASA, courtesy—cover *(top left; top right background; lunar rover);* pages 5, 6 *(inset);* 20, 21 *(Aldrin),* 32, 37, 42, 44–49, 51–56, 60–62, 64–70, 71 *(top),* 80, 82, 85, and 86

NASA, courtesy; photo by flight engineer Nikolai Budarin, International Space Station Expedition Six—page 73

NASA, courtesy; photo by David R. Scott—page 8

NASA, courtesy; photo by Robert Markowitz and Mark Sowa—page 19

NASA, courtesy; artwork by Pat Rawlings—page 75

©Photos.com—cover *(space shuttle, bottom left and top right);* pages 4, 6 *(background),* 12, 21 *(background),* 39 *(top),* 57, 59, and 93

Roddenberry family, courtesy—page 16

All other photos and illustrations not mentioned above are the property of or are protected by the Boy Scouts of America.

John McDearmon—all illustrations on pages 10, 13, 31, 38, and 71

Brian Payne—pages 22, 24, 25, and 26

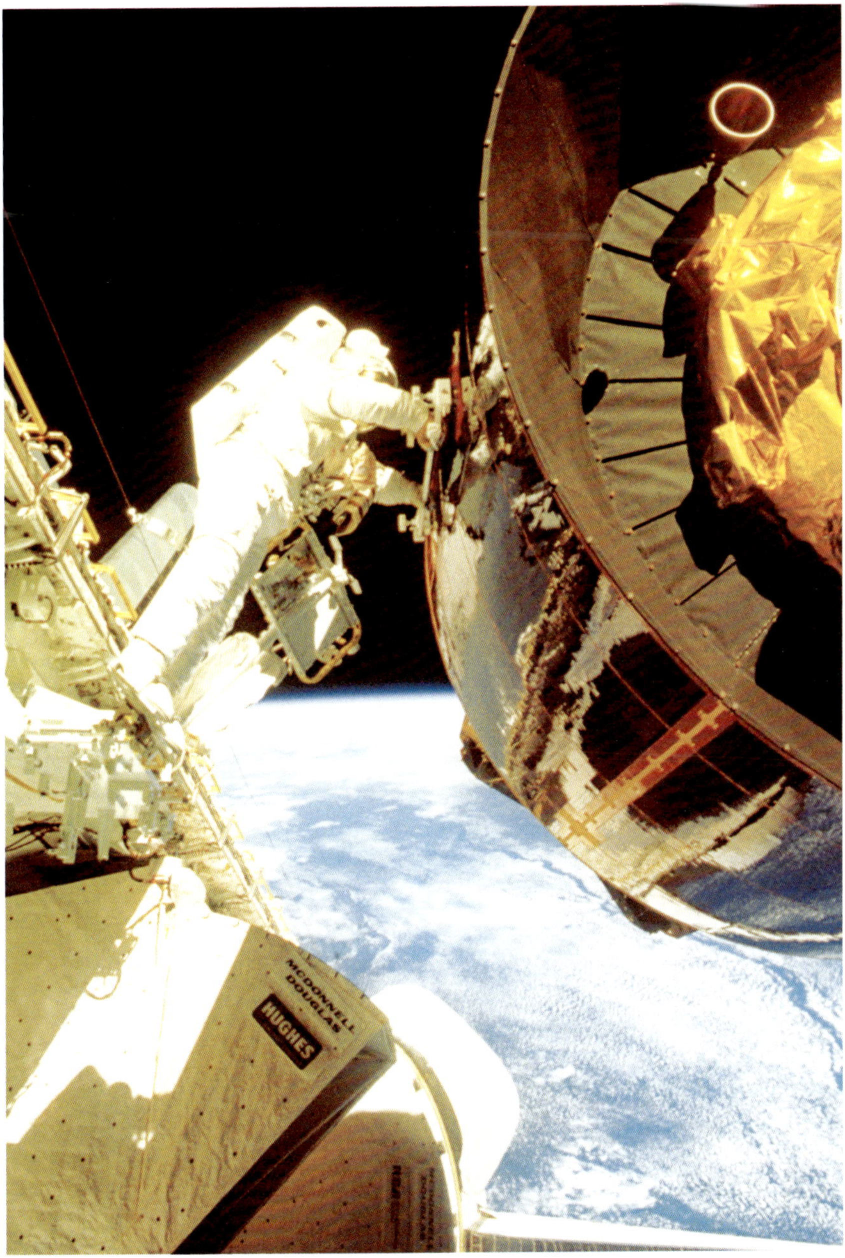
McDONNELL DOUGLAS
HUGHES

Notes

Notes

Notes